Keto Diet for Beginners 2018

Easy, Delicious and Healthy Keto Recipes to Heal Your Body, Shed Weight
and Regain Your Confidence (Lose up to 30 Pounds in 30 Days)

Suzanne Banks

Table of contents

INTRODUCTION

A standard ketogenic diet will try to limit your carbohydrate intake, keeping your protein intake moderate and increasing your fat content. So, it is safe to say that it would be 75% fats, 20% proteins, and 5% carbohydrates. There are different types of ketogenic diets:

- Cyclic: Ketogenic diet for 5 days with 2-day high carb break.
- Targeted: Consumption of carbs around workout.
- High-protein: Just has a higher protein content-35% than the standard one.

Why is ketogenic diet better than a low-fat diet? What is the main logic behind directing your body towards fat consumption? Whenever the body needs fuel, it turns to glucose, which is easier to access in the body and by limiting one's carb intake, one can train the body to switch to fats instead to function. The body gets its dose of glucose by breaking down carbohydrates in the digestive system. This way, your reservoir of fats can get a chance to get consumed. The ketogenic diet aims to put your body under ketosis. This is an interesting process that is discussed in Chapter 1. Usually, this state is achieved during fasting but this amazing diet, which you can follow indefinitely, can help you get there without the usual lethargy of fasting.

As the fats start getting consumed and your body is deprived of carbs, your body starts experiencing numerous healthy changes like lower insulin levels, controlled blood pressure, reduced appetite, etc.

People often question the viability of this diet because of the high-fat content. Anybody who wants to lose fat would be careful consuming fats because it is the accepted norm since the 1970s when the research at that time declared that saturated fats are bad. New research, however, disagrees with this concept and dispels the notion that consuming saturated fats can make your heart sick. Ketogenic diet does not only emphasize upon high fat consumption but low carb as well, and this balance is what people need to understand in order to understand the philosophy behind the diet.

This book will answer your queries about the effectiveness of the diet, its benefits, tips, detailed meal plans and recipes to set you off this new, healthy journey with confidence.

CHAPTER 1 - IS KETO RIGHT FOR YOU?

It's impossible to believe these days if someone has not heard of the ketogenic diet. It's a fad that is getting recognition and results- how can someone who is trying to lose weight or achieve a healthier lifestyle not be interested in knowing more about it. A simple Google search would reveal facts that will blow your mind. This is a celebrity endorsed diet and it got a place in the top 10 most Googled diets of 2017. All this popularity is good, but one is still allowed to be suspicious about its credibility, whether or not it is dangerous, effective enough and doable in the long run.

What Happens in Your Body When You Eat Keto?

The body goes into a state of ketosis, yes that is where the name of the diet comes from. This is the name of the process that your body undergoes for the fat break down to produce energy. The liver produces ketones, a type of acid which is then used to process the fats. Now ketones are very useful for your body; optimum levels can help you reduce your weight and give you several mental and physical benefits. This new regime shifts the body from its glycolysis mechanism to lipolysis.

How to Know Whether You Are in Ketosis

There are some telltale signs that one should look for in order to be sure that one is under ketosis

- **Feeling extra thirsty and less hungry** - This means that your sodium level is low, and your body needs more water in order to replenish the loss of electrolytes. The loss of appetite is because the diet reduces hunger hormones in the body
- **Losing weight in the first week** - Take this as a good sign that your diet is working. This is basically the water weight which reduces bloating
- **Bad breath** - Do not worry, this is the smell of the ketones that your body has not adapted to yet. Use mints to avoid embarrassment.
- **Higher ketone levels in blood, breath, and urine** - Any blood test, breath analyzer or urine test can measure the ketone levels in your body and give you the satisfaction that the diet is working
- **Fatigue in the beginning** - Do not get scared if you experience this initial loss of energy which is actually due to loss of electrolytes. Take it as a sign that your body is slowly adapting. After this initial lazy period, you will notice a peak in energy and focus because brain activity is boosted by ketone production
- **Trouble falling asleep** - This happens because carbs are responsible for making you feel sleepy. If you take that away, you get restless
- **Digestion problem** - You might experience constipation or diarrhea in the beginning as the body adapts to the high-fat diet, but this will slowly get better after the early stage.

CHAPTER2: WHAT IS BENEFITS FOR YOU WHEN YOU GO KETO?

Sustainable energy and body cleanse

During the first few days, you will feel very tired and will need to keep giving your body a steady supply of water and salts so that your body doesn't get dehydrated. After your body adjusts, you will feel a noticeable change in your energy levels as your body would have tapped into a new reserve of energy. So, by following this diet, you can cleanse your body and become more energetic as well.

Weight loss

Due to the low-carb diet, dieters experience a sharp drop in their body weight because the kidney loses sodium as insulin levels drop. Weight loss through keto diet is proven to be more than in other diets in the first six months.

Reduced appetite

One would think that following a low-fat diet would be a better option for losing weight, but low-carb diet works even better as the consumption of fat and protein satiates your hunger much quicker and you feel full. Hence, your calorie consumption is much lesser, and you do not feel miserable following this diet. This is what makes the diet doable.

Controlling Triglycerides levels

We are all aware of how triglycerides increase the risk of heart failure. These are the fat molecules that disrupt the blood flow and wreak havoc on your heart health. Controlling your carb consumption can significantly control triglyceride levels.

More good cholesterol

Good cholesterol, also known as High-density lipoprotein, is good for you because it takes fat from around the bod to the liver where it can be processed. This is good for cardiac health.

Blood sugar and insulin levels are reduced

Blood sugar level increases when we consume too many carbohydrates- they are broken down and enter the bloodstream as simple sugars. High blood sugar level can be lethal, and it is even more dangerous for people with type 2 diabetes as they have insulin resistance. Insulin is the hormone that controls sudden spikes in sugar levels. Studies have proved that this diet can control and reverse type 2 diabetes.

Controlling High Blood Pressure

Hypertension is a problem for a lot of people as it risks heart disease, stroke, and kidney failure so following this low-carb diet can shield you from these horrible diseases.

Improvement in LDL (Low-Density Lipoprotein)

LDL is commonly known as bad cholesterol. The kind of cholesterol that makes one prone to all sorts of heart diseases. Luckily, scientists have discovered a solution to reduce its bad impact by making the smaller particles bigger. The dietary changes in keto make LDL go through this pattern change and also reduce the number of particles in the bloodstream so you can have a healthy heart.

Effects on brain health

The ketogenic diet was first introduced in the early 90s for epileptic patients. They were able to go off medication and find a cure for their seizures through this diet. The brain needs glucose to burn in order to function smoothly, but it can also function by burning ketones. Besides epilepsy, it can also help with autism, Parkinson's disease, Alzheimer's, migraines, etc.

Skin care

High carb diet can cause acne to act up so following this clean diet will help reduce lesions and inflammation

CHAPTER 3: FOODS TO EAT

Let us now review now all the foods that you are allowed to eat during this eat. It is not very restrictive and there is a variety of foods you can consume to achieve ketosis state. Remember that you have to stay within 20-50 grams of carbs per day. Here are some foods you can have to meet these criteria:

1. Meat: Meat is allowed but you can only eat in a limited amount. Grass-fed meat should be preferred over grain-fed as it is less nutritious. Fresh meat, which is a source of high-quality protein, is very important for maintaining muscle mass during this diet. Dairy products like milk, yogurt, butter, and cream, as long as they are full-fat items are also allowed. Eggs are ideal because they make you feel full and they have the right amount of fat and protein as well, 1 gram of carbs and less than 6 grams of protein. Do not leave the yolk out as it contains most of the egg's nutrients like lutein and zeaxanthin. It does not shoot your cholesterol either.

2. Seafood is good too: Some famous seafoods you can consume without being afraid of messing up your diet are fish and shellfish. You have to vary about the kind of shellfish and fish you choose- Salmon, for example, is safe because it is carb-free and so are shellfish like shrimp, clams, mussels, octopus, oysters, and squid. Consumption of this seafood will also help you lower insulin levels and improve mental health due to the amount vitamins, minerals, and omega-3s.

3. Fruits that are allowed: All fruits are allowed because they are sugary and have a high carb content. This includes tropical fruits, syrups, concentrates and smoothies made from these fruits, but berries are safe. They are low in carbs and high in fiber. Some berries you can consume are raspberries, blackberries, blueberries, and strawberries. Blueberries have the highest, about 12 grams, amount of net carbs.

4. Vegetables that are low in carbs: Go for non-starchy vegetables since one serving of those won't cross your daily carb limit. This includes spinach, cauliflower, zucchini, and squash. These vegetables have low calories and carbs, but they are rich in vitamin C and minerals.

5. Cheese: Cheese is perfect for keto diet since it has low carb and high fat count. Do not be afraid, it does not cause risk of heart disease because of its saturated fat content. In fact, the conjugated linoleic acid present in cheese is good for losing fat and

gaining strength. You can try ricotta or cheddar as these are both good sources of protein, calcium and good fatty acids.

6. Avocados: Isn't it surprising that 100 grams of avocado contains only 2 grams of the net carb? This is an excellent supplement of potassium as well which helps you get used to the diet.

7. Coconut oil and olive oil: Ketones are made from medium-chain triglycerides in the liver and coconut oil is abundant in these long-chain fats. It is also helpful in losing weight, especially belly fat. This makes it a perfect oil for this diet. Another oil that you can use is olive oil, preferably, extra-virgin olive oil. It is good for your heart, contains antioxidants and contains absolutely no carbs so you can use it for your salads without worry. It is also safe to use it for low heat cooking).

8. Greek yogurt: This is also a good food for making you feel full and it is also very yummy. Throw some nuts and cinnamon for a nice snack.

9. Nuts and seeds are amazing: These are amazing because of the high-fat and low-carb content. They are versatile and can be garnished over any dessert or dish. They make your stomach feel full due to the high fiber content. Use all the almonds, cashews, macadamia nuts, pecans, pistachios, walnuts, flax seeds, chia seeds around your house without hesitation when you are following this diet.

10. Hot beverages: Of course, you will feel the need to have coffee and tea during the day. These are healthy and carb-free, and the caffeine is good for your alertness as well but try your best to stay away from sweetened and non-fat milk drinks. Some fun drinks to try while you're on keto are acai almond butter smoothie, micronutrient greens matcha smoothie, chocolate sea salt smoothie and perfect keto Frappuccino.

CHAPTER 4: FOODS TO AVOID

There are some foods that you have to be careful you do not consume during your diet as extra carb and protein can bring you out of ketosis. We first looked at foods that can help you bring in ketosis, now let us take a look at the foods you must avoid for your diet's success:

1. **Grains:** These are known to have a lot of carbs and should be avoided at all cost so do not eat any grains, whole grain or sprouted grains.
2. **Bread:** Bread is also a byproduct of grain, so it is understandable why this is prohibited.
3. **Pasta:** Pasta is quick to cook and tasty, but you will have to stay off it while you are on keto as it is, sadly, made from a grain as well
4. **Beans and legumes:** Although canned beans or boiled beans are a good option for when you come back from work, it will not help you while you are on keto diet as they contain a high amount of starch.
5. **Fruits to avoid:** One might think fruits will be helpful when trying to have a healthier lifestyle, but ketogenic diet demands that you stay off carbs which means sugary fruits as well. Tropical fruits, syrups, concentrates, and smoothies from all such fruits should be avoided.
6. **Vegetables to avoid:** This is tricky one but here is a rule of thumb that will help you stay in the clear: avoid vegetables that grow beneath the ground as they are high in starch.
7. **Oils to use:** Use of some kinds of oils is encouraged in the keto diet and they have been discussed at length in the last chapter. You must avoid processed oils like canola oil, peanut oil, corn oil, sesame oil in your food.
8. **Meats to avoid:** When buying meat, you have to be careful about the source of the meat as the nutritious value might not be what you think it is when you buy it. To stay away from such dubious meat sources, avoid buying factory-farmed fish and pork and processed meat like hot dogs, packed sausages, etc.
9. **Alcohol:** This is hard for a lot of people, but it should be emphasized here that consumption of alcohol can slow down the rate of fat loss and increase carbs in the body, which is bad news for followers of a keto diet. Hard liquor is better than all kinds of beers, wines, cocktails, mixers with flavorings and flavored liquors but even that can be bad if you are trying to stay in your carb limit.

10. Sugary drinks: As discussed in the hot beverages section of the previous chapter, sugary drinks are bad for your keto diet. They are full of carbs and can imbalance your ketosis. These sugary drinks include sodas even diet sodas as well, fruit juices even if they are freshly extracted, fruit and vegetable smoothies and sweet milk drinks.

11. Sweeteners: Sweeteners can be dangerous because they can make you crave more and hence, disturb your self-discipline. You must avoid all kinds of artificial sweeteners like Equal, Splenda, Aspartame, Saccharin, Sucralose, Acesulfame, etc.

12. Packaged food: Most packaged snacks are full of extra sugar, trans-fats, and preservatives but people mostly consume them mindlessly. Some things that you must avoid on your keto diet are commercially baked goods, ice cream, margarine, candies, wheat gluten, foods with carrageenan, sulfites, unhealthy oils, etc. Do not be fooled by the 'low fat' label either.

CHAPTER 5: THE COMMON MISTAKES FOR BEGINNERS

There are some common rookie mistakes that everyone who is new to the keto diet makes unknowingly and in order to avoid that, every beginner should educate himself or herself about these mistakes to avoid them. Starting a new diet is daunting and requires a strong willpower and you have to be ready for all the changes you will go through- mentally and physically- during the course of the initial stage. Here are some guidelines that you should follow in order to avoid over-consuming or under consuming your daily nutrients:

- Carbohydrate intake should be 35 to 50 grams. This is roughly equal to 20 grams of pure carbs per day.

- 1.4 to 1.7 grams of protein per kg of body weight is acceptable. This is important to know since over-consumption of protein can cause your body to convert that extra protein into glucose which can disturb your ketosis

- You must consume 2.5 liters of water every day. It has to stay between 3 to 4 liters per day.

Even though sugary snacks are easy and fun to eat, you should resist the urge to consume too many in order to stay within the mentioned carb limits. Periodic fasting is not a good idea if your body is not ready for the rigorous starvation demanded by the process, you can increase your ketone levels in other ways as well. As for exercise, it is a very good way of increasing your fat burning rate. Try 20 to 30 minutes of training with weight lifting to achieve desired results.

When you are new on the diet, you will feel lethargic which is very common, and you should not be scared of it. Nausea is a common effect as well. These sudden discomforts can throw a beginner off, but one should take it as a good sign that the diet is working because it shows that your body is getting used to the fat burning for fuel production. You might even experience the 'keto flu' but you can overcome this by extra water and salt consumption. One way to do that is by having chicken broth regularly. Your body loses water because carb consumption is limited, and the body starts consuming glycogen, which causes water loss from the body. Hence it is important to avoid dehydration. You can find more helpful information in the later chapters about meal plans and tasty recipes. Meal planning is a very important aspect of this diet in order to keep the daily macros limits in check.

During the adaptation period, do not load yourself up on keto-friendly food. Eat slowly and in moderation. Smaller meals should be taken often with an emphasis on soluble fibers and low-calorie vegetables. Fat consumption should be increased after a month but prior to that, keep it to a very moderate amount.

Everyone's body is different, and people tend to get carried away by looking at success stories online of people losing weight due to their success with the ketogenic diet. This is not something a beginner should be obsessing over. Person A's body might lose fat and it shows clearly on the scales while person B's waist might be reducing without any measurable evidence on the scales. So, one must not judge the success of the diet by weight loss comparison as it will only discourage from following through with the diet.

It is important to stress here that keto is a lifestyle rather than a diet even though people go to it in order to lose weight. There are many other ways to lose weight and they are quick fixes, but keto demands a little more patience and commitment as you cannot quit it and start following the diet you used to follow before the diet. All the results you achieve will be lost if you abandon it so quickly and without care.

Another thing that is ignored commonly is the sleep cycle. You should get an ample amount of sleep during the night so that you do not get carb cravings in the morning.

Adjusting to keto is hard and you should get your friends involved or get in touch with people online who are trying to follow the diet and share experiences to have a 'keto camaraderie'.

CHAPTER 6: CAN I WORK OUT ON KETO DIET?

Since keto followers would assume that fat loss is guaranteed without any extra effort during the diet, it is important to discuss this point and clarify whether this is the way to go or some kind of exercise regimen should be followed.

The main concern that people have is that carb consumption is important for a successful workout whereas the very gist of the keto diet is to avoid carbs in all forms. So where will your body get its extra energy from? There is no need to lose your calm about this as you are allowed to eat a little number of carbs to kick-start your workout, but this will not affect your keto carb balance. You must be warned here that working out during the adaptation period is not a good idea.

You can stay active and healthy during your keto diet- your performance will not be affected by the restrictive diet.

CHAPTER 7: FAQs

1. Do ketone levels need to be measured?

   It is recommended that you do get your ketone levels checked at the beginning of the diet but there is no need to keep checking them obsessively throughout the course of the diet and after you have adapted.

2. What is a good way to measure carbs and macros?

   There are apps on the web that can help you measure these successfully

3. Is keeping track of calories important?

   This becomes important if you are not being able to lose your weight within 2 to 3 weeks of the diet as the diet automatically suppresses your appetite to the point that overconsumption of calories does not remain an issue. You can do it using an app.

4. Is muscle build up possible during the diet?

   Yes, this is possible, and you can read up further about it online.

5. What are some dangers of ketosis?

   There are no dangers of ketosis. Natural ketosis is different from ketoacidosis which is a medical condition

6. Is High BMI unhealthy?

   BMI can be misleading because it only compares your body weight and height, it just not take into account the body composition and how much of the weight is actually body fat. High BMI does not translate into unhealthy.

7. Are fiber supplements required to fight diarrhea and constipation?

   Restraining your grain and fruit intake is not going to limit your fiber intake, you can consume it through vegetables, nuts and some fruits that are allowed on the diet. In cases of diarrhea and constipation, drink more water, keep an eye on mineral intake and stay active.

8. Can vegans try this diet?

   Being a vegan and follower of keto diet are two different things. However, a vegetarian can easily go on a keto diet.

9. How should one incorporate cheat days?

You should not have cheat days during the starting period while you are losing your water weight as it does not help in tracking the amount of weight loss.

10. Please tell how intermittent fasting can be followed

It is not recommended during the first four weeks of the diet when it is getting adapted to the keto diet.

11. Desserts in keto?

It can be difficult for followers of the keto diet to quit sugary snacks all of a sudden, especially for the ones who have sweet tooth. You can use low carb sweeteners like stevia, monk fruit powder, etc. but do get rid of all the sugary prohibited food when you start the diet.

CHAPTER8: MEAL PLAN

Now let's take a look at the low-carb meals. The goal of any keto meal is simplicity and keeping this notion in mind, a healthy 3 weeks meal plan is designed. In chapter 9, you will detail preparations for each recipe. Check out the meal plan below.

WEEK 1

MONDAY –

- For Breakfast: Cheesy Spinach Omelet
- For Lunch: Lemon Garlic Pork Steaks
- For Snack: Roasted Cauliflower Hummus
- For Dinner: Meatloaf
- For Dessert: Macadamia Nut Fat Bomb

TUESDAY –

- For Breakfast: Baked Eggs in Avocado
- For Lunch: Lamb Slider Patties
- For Snack: Brussels Sprout Chips
- For Dinner: Pork Stroganoff
- For Dessert: Macadamia Nut Fat Bomb

WEDNESDAY –

- For Breakfast: Baked Eggs in Avocado
- For Lunch: Coffee-Chipotle Pork Chops

- For Snack: Tuna Pickle Boats

- For Dinner: Stuffed Bacon Cheeseburger

- For Dessert: Macadamia Nut Fat Bomb

THURSDAY –

- For Breakfast: Coconut Porridge

- For Lunch: No-Noodle Chicken Soup

- For Snack: Cream Cheese Stuffed Peppers

- For Dinner: Egg Roll in a Bowl

- For Dessert: Mug Cake

FRIDAY –

- For Breakfast: Coconut Porridge

- For Lunch: Avocado Tuna Salad

- For Snack: Lamb & Leek Burgers with Lemon Cream

- For Dinner: Chicken Carbonara

- For Dessert: Coconut Bars

SATURDAY –

- For Breakfast: Coconut Porridge

- For Lunch: Chicken Caesar Salad

- For Snack: Bacon Avocado Bombs

- For Dinner: Pepperoni Pizza

- For Dessert: Coconut Bars

SUNDAY –

- For Breakfast: Spinach Frittata
- For Lunch: Fried Chicken
- For Snack: Smoked Salmon Appetizer
- For Dinner: Lamb Curry
- For Dessert: Coconut Bars

WEEK 2

MONDAY –

- For Breakfast: Mushroom Omelet
- For Lunch: Shrimps & Artichoke
- For Snack: Brussels Sprout Chips
- For Dinner: Cheesesteak Casserole
- For Dessert: Chocolate Mousse

TUESDAY –

- For Breakfast: Mushroom Omelet
- For Lunch: Mackerel Salad
- For Snack: Onion Rings
- For Dinner: Pork & Noodle Stir Fry
- For Dessert: Avocado Vanilla Pudding

WEDNESDAY –

- For Breakfast: Pancakes

- For Lunch: White Turkey Chili

- For Snack: Salmon Stuffed Avocado

- For Dinner: Jalapeno Shrimp Veggies Bake

- For Dessert: No Bake Cookies

THURSDAY –

- For Breakfast: Scrambled eggs

- For Lunch: Jerk Chicken

- For Snack: Salmon Stuffed Avocado

- For Dinner: Pecan Crusted Rack of Lamb

- For Dessert: No Bake Cookies

FRIDAY –

- For Breakfast: Scrambled eggs

- For Lunch: Chicken Fajita Soup

- For Snack: Roasted Cauliflower Hummus

- For Dinner: Cheesy Salmon with Broccoli

- For Dessert: No Bake Cookies

SATURDAY –

- For Breakfast: Scrambled eggs

- For Lunch: Zuppa Toscana Soup

- For Snack: Mug Bread

- For Dinner: Mushroom Chicken

- For Dessert: No Bake Cookies

SUNDAY –

- For Breakfast: Zucchini Breakfast Hash

- For Lunch: Pepperoni Pizza

- For Snack: Cream Cheese Stuffed Peppers

- For Dinner: Lemon Chicken

- For Dessert: Lemon Bars

WEEK 3

MONDAY –

- For Breakfast: Zucchini Breakfast Hash

- For Lunch: Turkey Sausage Frittata

- For Snack: Roasted Cauliflower Hummus

- For Dinner: Fish Casserole

- For Dessert: Coconut Bars

TUESDAY –

- For Breakfast: Baked Eggs in Avocado

- For Lunch: Taco Soup

- For Snack: Fried Chicken

- For Dinner: Paprika Chicken

- For Dessert: Lemon Barss

WEDNESDAY –

- For Breakfast: Coconut Porridge

- For Lunch: Avocado & Egg Salad

- For Snack: Mug Bread

- For Dinner: Paprika Chicken

- For Dessert: Chocolate Mousse

THURSDAY –

- For Breakfast: Coconut Porridge

- For Lunch: Mexican Chicken Soup

- For Snack: Salmon Stuffed Avocado

- For Dinner: Clams Italiano

- For Dessert: Chocolate Bark with Bacon and Almonds

FRIDAY –

- For Breakfast: Scrambled eggs

- For Lunch: Paprika Chicken

- For Snack: Tuna Pickle Boats

- For Dinner: Lamb Curry

- For Dessert: Chocolate Bark with Bacon and Almonds

SATURDAY –

- For Breakfast: Pancakes

- For Lunch: Beef Stroganoff Soup

- For Snack: Mug Bread

- For Dinner: Thai fish & Coconut Curry

- For Dessert: Chocolate Bark with Bacon and Almonds

SUNDAY –

- For Breakfast: Scrambled eggs

- For Lunch: Chicken Tenders

- For Snack: Onion Rings

- For Dinner: Salmon Steaks

- For Dessert: Mug Cake

CHAPTER 9: BREAKFAST RECIPES

Cheesy Spinach Omelet

Servings: 1 omelet.
Preparation time: 10 minutes
Cooking time: 25 hours
Total time: 35 minutes

Nutrition Value:
Calories: 529 Cal, Carbs: 6 g, Net Carbs: 5.35 g, Fat: 41.8 g, Protein: 31.4 g, Fiber: 0.7 g.

Ingredients:

- 2 breakfast sausage, small-sized
- 1 cup baby spinach, fresh
- 1/2 teaspoon salt
- 1/4 teaspoon ground black pepper
- ½ tablespoon olive oil
- 1 tablespoon crumbled feta cheese
- 3 eggs, lightly whisked
- ¼ cup half-and-half

Method:

1. Place a skillet pan over medium heat, let heat and then add sausages.
2. Let cook for 4 to 5 minutes or until cooked through.
3. In the meantime, crack eggs in a bowl and whisk in half-and-half along with 1/8 teaspoon of each salt and black pepper.
4. When sausage is cooked, transfer to a plate lined with paper towels.
5. Clean the pan, then add oil and when heated, add spinach to pan.
6. Season with remaining salt and black pepper and let cook for 5 minutes or until spinach leaves wilts.
7. Then transfer spinach to a sausage plate and pour in prepared egg mixture.
8. Let cook until bottom sets completely and start to get cooked.

9. Then scatter with sausage, spinach leaves and cheese on top.
10. Carefully flip the omelet and let cook for 1 minute.
11. Then flip half omelet onto the other side and continue cooking for 3 minutes.
12. Flip again, then cover with another pan, and let cook for 3 to 5 minutes or until omelet is cooked through.
13. When done, slide omelet onto a serving platter and serve.

Baked Eggs in Avocado

Servings: 6 avocados.
Preparation time: 10 minutes
Cooking time: 18 minutes
Total time: 28 minutes

Nutrition Value:
Calories: 231.6 Cal, Carbs: 9.5 g, Net Carbs: 2.7 g, Fat: 19.7 g, Protein: 7.9 g, Fiber: 6.8 g.

Ingredients:

- 3 avocados, halved and cored
- ¾ teaspoon salt, divided
- ¾ teaspoon ground black pepper, divided
- 2 tablespoons chopped chives
- 6 eggs

Method:

1. Set oven to 425 degrees F and let preheat.
2. Take a large baking sheet and grease with non-stick cooking spray.
3. Scoop out about 2 tablespoons of avocado flesh to create a well in avocado and place onto baking sheet, well side up.
4. Crack an egg into each well and then sprinkle with 1/8 teaspoon of salt and black pepper.
5. Place the baking sheet into the oven and let bake for 15 to 18 minutes or until egg whites are set.
6. When done, remove avocado from the oven and serve immediately.

Scrambled eggs

Servings: 1 plate.
Preparation time: 5 minutes
Cooking time: 5 hours
Total time: 10 minutes

Nutrition Value:
Calories: 237 Cal, Carbs: 3 g, Net Carbs: 1 g, Fat: 31 g, Protein: 34 g, Fiber: 2 g.

Ingredients:

- ¼ teaspoon salt
- ¼ teaspoon ground black pepper
- 2 tablespoons unsalted butter
- 2 eggs

Method:

1. Crack eggs in a bowl, add salt and black pepper and whisk until combined.
2. Place a skillet pan over medium heat, add butter and when melted, pour in egg mixture.
3. Stir for 1 to 2 minutes or until mixture turns creamy.
4. Then transfer eggs to a plate and serve.

Spinach Frittata

Servings: 4 slices.
Preparation time: 10 minutes
Cooking time: 40 minutes
Total time: 50 minutes

Nutrition Value:
Calories: 661 Cal, Carbs: 7 g, Net Carbs: 4 g, Fat: 59 g, Protein: 27 g, Fiber: 3 g.

Ingredients:

- 5-ounce diced bacon
- 8-ounce baby spinach
- 1 ½ teaspoon salt
- 1 teaspoon ground black pepper
- 2 tablespoons unsalted butter
- 5-ounce shredded cheddar cheese
- 1 cup heavy whipping cream
- 8 eggs

Method:

1. Set oven to 350 degrees F and let preheat.
2. In the meantime, place a skillet pan over medium-high heat, add bacon and let cook for 5 minutes or until crispy.
3. Then stir in spinach and continue cooking for 3 to 4 minutes or until wilts.
4. When done, remove the pan from heat and set aside until required.
5. Crack eggs in a bowl, then whisk in cream, salt, and black pepper and pour this mixture into square baking dish.
6. Top evenly with prepared spinach mixture and then scatter with cheese.
7. Place baking dish into the oven and let bake for 25 to 30 minutes or until top is golden brown and frittata is set.
8. Slice to serve.

Mushroom Omelet

Servings: 1 omelet.
Preparation time: 5 minutes
Cooking time: 8 minutes
Total time: 12 minutes

Nutrition Value:
Calories: 510 Cal, Carbs: 5 g, Net Carbs: 4 g, Fat: 3 g, Protein: 25 g, Fiber: 1 g.

Ingredients:

- 3 tablespoons chopped white onion
- 3 mushrooms
- ½ teaspoon salt
- ½ teaspoon ground black pepper
- 2 tablespoons unsalted butter
- 3 eggs
- 2 tablespoons shredded cheddar cheese

Method:

1. Crack eggs in a bowl and whisk in salt, black pepper until smooth.
2. Place a frying pan over medium heat, add butter and when melts, pour in prepared egg mixture.
3. Let cook for 3 minutes or until starting to get firm.
4. Then sprinkle onion, mushroom, and cheese on top of omelet and then carefully fold one half of omelet to other.
5. When bottom turns golden brown, slide omelet to a serving plate and serve.

Pancakes

Servings: 4 pancakes.
Preparation time: 5 minutes
Cooking time: 20
Total time: 25 minutes

Nutrition Value:
Calories: 425 Cal, Carbs: 8 g, Net Carbs: 5 g, Fat: 39 g, Protein: 13 g, Fiber: 3 g.

Ingredients:

- 25 teaspoons raspberries
- 1 tablespoons ground husk powder
- 4 tablespoons unsalted butter
- 1 cup heavy whipping cream
- 1 cup crumbled cottage cheese
- 4 eggs

Method:

1. Crack eggs in a bowl and stir in husk powder and cheese until mixed, and then let rest for 10 minutes or until thickened.
2. Then place skillet pan over medium heat, add butter and when melt, pour in a ¼ portion of prepared pancake mixture.
3. Smooth the top using a spatula and let cook for 3 to 4 minutes per side or until nicely golden brown.
4. Cook remaining pancakes in the same manner.
5. Whisk whipping cream until soft peaks form and serve pancakes with cream and berries.

Coconut Porridge

Servings: 1 bowl.
Preparation time: 5 minutes
Cooking time: 15 minutes
Total time: 20 minutes

Nutrition Value:
Calories: 486 Cal, Carbs: 9 g, Net Carbs: 4 g, Fat: 49 g, Protein: 9 g, Fiber: 5 g.

Ingredients:

- 1 tablespoons coconut flour
- 1/8 teaspoon ground husk powder
- 1/8 teaspoon salt
- 4 tablespoons coconut cream
- 2 tablespoons unsalted butter
- 1 egg

Method:

1. Place all ingredients in a saucepan and mix well.
2. Then place the pan over low heat and let cook until porridge reaches to desired consistency, stirring constantly.
3. When done, spoon porridge into a bowl and serve with cream and favorite sliced fruit.

Zucchini Breakfast Hash

Servings: 1 plate.
Preparation time: 5 minutes
Cooking time: 25 minutes
Total time: 30 minutes

Nutrition Value:
Calories: 423 Cal, Carbs: 9.1 g, Net Carbs: 6.6 g, Fat: 35.5 g, Protein: 17.4 g, Fiber: 2.5 g.

Ingredients:

- 2 slices of bacon, diced
- 1 medium-sized zucchini, trimmed and diced
- 1 tablespoon chopped parsley
- 1 teaspoon minced garlic
- 1/4 teaspoon salt
- 1 tablespoon olive oil
- 1 egg

Method:

1. Place a skillet pan over medium heat, add garlic and let cook for 2 to 3 minutes or until fragrant and nicely golden brown.
2. Then add bacon and continue cooking for 3 to 5 minutes or until nicely golden brown.
3. Stir in zucchini and continue cooking for 12 to 15 minutes or until cooked through.
4. When done, remove the pan from heat and sprinkle with parsley.
5. Fry egg up to your desired taste, then top it over zucchini hash and serve.

CHAPTER 10: APPETIZER & SNACKS

Lamb & Leek Burgers with Lemon Cream

Servings: 4 burgers.
Preparation time: 10 minutes
Cooking time: 15 minutes
Total time: 25 minutes

Nutrition Value:
Calories: 170 Cal, Carbs: 1.6 g, Net Carbs: 0.6 g, Fat: 8 g, Protein: 23 g, Fiber: 1 g.

Ingredients:

- 16-ounce ground lamb
- 4 large lettuce leaves
- 1/2 cup chopped leeks
- 1/2 tablespoon garlic powder
- 1/2 teaspoon sea salt
- 1 tablespoon lemon zest
- 1 tablespoon coconut oil
- ½ cup coconut cream

Method:

1. Place a skillet pan over medium heat, add ½ teaspoon oil and when heated, add leeks.
2. Let cook for 3 to 5 minutes or until softened, then transfer to a bowl and let cool at room temperature.
3. Place ground meat in another bowl and add garlic powder and salt.
4. Add cooled leeks and mix until combined.
5. The shaped mixture into four patties.
6. Return skillet over medium-low heat, add remaining oil and add patties in it.
7. Let cook for 5 minutes per side or until cooked through.

8. In the meantime, place coconut cream and lemon zest in a blender and pulse until combined.

9. Place each patty in a large lettuce leaf, top with prepared cream dressing, then fold and serve.

Salmon Stuffed Avocado

Servings: 2.
Preparation time: 15 minutes
Cooking time: 25 minutes
Total time: 40 minutes

Nutrition Value:
Calories: 463 Cal, Carbs: 13.9 g, Net Carbs: 6.4 g, Fat: 34.6 g, Protein: 27 g, Fiber: 7.5 g.

Ingredients:

- 8-ounce salmon fillets, cooked
- 1 large avocado, cored
- 1 tablespoon chopped dill
- 1 small white onion, peeled and chopped
- ¾ teaspoon salt
- ½ teaspoon ground black pepper
- 2 tablespoons lemon juice
- 1 tablespoon coconut oil
- 1/4 cup soured cream
- lemon wedges for garnish

Method:

1. Set oven to 400 degrees F and let preheat.
2. In the meantime, take a baking tray, line with parchment sheet and place salmon fillets on it.
3. Drizzle with coconut oil and 1 tablespoon lemon juice and season with salt and black pepper.
4. Place the baking tray into the oven and let bake for 25 minutes or until cooked through.
5. When done, remove salmon from oven, let cool for 10 minutes and then shred using a fork, discarding skin.
6. Place shredded salmon in a bowl and add onion, cream, dill and lemon juice.

7. Stir until combined and then taste to adjust salt and black pepper.
8. Cut avocado into half, remove its pit and then scoop out about 1-inch avocado flesh using an ice cream scoop.
9. Cut scoop out avocado into small pieces, add to salmon mixture, stir until mixed and then fill prepared salmon mixture into that hollow.
10. Drizzle with lemon juice and serve.

Smoked Salmon Appetizer

Servings: 6.
Preparation time: 20 minutes
Cooking time: 0 minute
Total time: 20 minutes

Nutrition Value:
Calories: 330 Cal, Carbs: 3 g, Net Carbs: 3 g, Fat: 26 g, Protein: 23 g, Fiber: 0 g.

Ingredients:

- 7-ounce smoked salmon
- 2-ounce small lettuce leaves
- ¼ teaspoon ground black pepper
- 4 tablespoons chopped dill
- 2 tablespoons lemon zest
- 8-ounce cream cheese
- 15 teaspoon sour cream

Method:

1. Cut salmon into small even pieces and then place in a large bowl.
2. Add remaining ingredients to a bowl except for lettuce and stir until well mixed.
3. Let this mixture sit for 15 minutes.
4. Then fill lettuce leaves with the prepared salmon mixture and serve.

Roasted Cauliflower Hummus

Servings: 4.
Preparation time: 15 minutes
Cooking time: 40 minutes
Total time: 55 minutes

Nutrition Value:
Calories: 40 Cal, Carbs: 2 g, Net Carbs: 1 g, Fat: 4 g, Protein: 1 g, Fiber: 1 g.

Ingredients:

- 1 medium-sized head of cauliflower
- 1 clove of garlic, peeled
- 1 lemon, cut into wedges
- 2 tablespoons chopped parsley
- 1 teaspoon salt
- ¾ teaspoon ground black pepper
- 1/3 cup tahini paste
- 2 tablespoons lemon juice
- 3 tablespoons olive oil, divided
- Vegetable slices for serving

Method:

1. Set oven to 400 degrees F and let preheat.
2. Take a large rimmed baking sheet, grease with non-stick cooking spray.
3. Cut cauliflower into florets and then arrange on a baking sheet in a single layer.
4. Drizzle with 2 tablespoons oil and then place baking sheet into the oven.
5. Let bake for 40 minutes or until roasted, stirring halfway through.
6. When done, remove baking sheet from oven and let cool on wire rack.
7. Then transfer cauliflower florets in a food processor and add garlic, salt, black pepper, tahini paste, lemon juice and olive oil.
8. Pulse for 2 minutes or until smooth and tip hummus in a bowl.

9. Drizzle with olive oil, sprinkle with parsley and serve with lemon wedges and vegetable slices.

Brussels Sprout Chips

Servings: 3.
Preparation time: 10 minutes
Cooking time: 20 minutes
Total time: 30 minutes

Nutrition Value:
Calories: 296 Cal, Carbs: 12 g, Net Carbs: 8 g, Fat: 28 g, Protein: 4 g, Fiber: 4 g.

Ingredients:

- 8-ounce Brussels sprouts, thinly sliced
- 1 teaspoon garlic powder
- 1 teaspoon salt
- ¾ teaspoon ground black pepper
- 1 tablespoon olive oil
- 2 tablespoons grated Parmesan cheese

Method:

1. Set oven to 400 degrees F and let preheat.
2. Place slices of Brussels sprouts in a large bowl and drizzle with olive oil.
3. Add garlic powder, salt, black pepper and cheese and toss to evenly coat.
4. Spread Brussels sprouts in a single layer on a baking sheet and then place into the oven.
5. Let bake for 20 minutes, tossing halfway through, until nicely golden brown and crispy.
6. Serve with your favorite dipping sauce.

Cream Cheese Stuffed Peppers

Servings: 8 bell peppers.
Preparation time: 10 minutes
Cooking time: 20 minutes
Total time: 30 minutes

Nutrition Value:
Calories: 410 Cal, Carbs: 7 g, Net Carbs: 6 g, Fat: 37 g, Protein: 12 g, Fiber: 1 g.

Ingredients:

- 8-ounce small-sized bell peppers
- 1-ounce chorizo, chopped
- 1 tablespoon chopped cilantro
- 1 tablespoon chipotle paste
- 2 tablespoons olive oil
- 8-ounce cream cheese
- 1 cup grated parmesan cheese

Method:

1. Set oven to 400 degrees F and let preheat.
2. In the meantime, cut each bell pepper into half, lengthwise, and then remove its core.
3. Stir together all the ingredients except for parmesan cheese and then fill into peppers.
4. Take a baking sheet, line with non-stick cooking spray and place stuffed peppers on it.
5. Spread cheese onto each pepper and let bake for 15 to 20 minutes or until cheese melts and the top is nicely golden brown.

Bacon Avocado Bombs

Servings: 2 avocados.
Preparation time: 15 minutes
Cooking time: 5 minutes
Total time: 20 minutes

Nutrition Value:
Calories: 196 Cal, Carbs: 5 g, Net Carbs: 4 g, Fat: 19 g, Protein: 6 g, Fiber: 1 g.

Ingredients:

- 8 slices of bacon
- 2 medium-sized avocados, peeled and cored
- 1/3 cup grated cheddar cheese

Method:

1. Switch on the broiler and let preheat.
2. Take a small baking sheet, line with aluminum sheet and set aside until required.
3. Peel each avocado, then cut into half and remove its pit.
4. Fill hollows in avocado halves with cheese and then top each with unfilled avocado half.
5. Wrap avocados with bacon slices, 4 slices for each and then place onto the prepared baking sheet.
6. Place the baking sheet into the oven and let broil for 5 minutes or until top is crispy.
7. Then carefully flip avocados and continue broiling for 5 minutes or until crispy on all sides.
8. Serve straight away.

Tuna Pickle Boats

Servings: 12.
Preparation time: 15 minutes
Cooking time: 0 minutes
Total time: 15 minutes

Nutrition Value:
Calories: 108 Cal, Carbs: 1 g, Net Carbs: 0 g, Fat: 7 g, Protein: 9 g, Fiber: 1 g.

Ingredients:

- 5-ounce flaked tuna
- 6 dill pickles
- 1 tablespoon chopped dill and more as needed for garnish
- 1 teaspoon salt
- ¾ teaspoon ground black pepper
- 1/4 cup sour cream

Method:

1. Cut each pickle into the half, lengthwise and then scoop out its seed.
2. Drain tuna flakes, then place them in a bowl and add remaining ingredients.
3. Mix until combined and then fill into pickle halves.
4. Garnish filled pickles with dill and serve.

Onion Rings

Servings: 4.
Preparation time: 15 minutes
Cooking time: 15 minutes
Total time: 25 minutes

Nutrition Value:
Calories: 175 Cal, Carbs: 7 g, Net Carbs: 4 g, Fat: 16 g, Protein: 3 g, Fiber: 3 g.

Ingredients:

- 2-ounce pork rinds
- ½ cup coconut flour
- 1 medium-sized white onion, peeled
- 2 eggs, slightly beaten
- 1 tablespoon whipping cream
- 1/2 cup grated parmesan cheese

Method:

1. Set oven for 425 degrees F and let preheat.
2. Cut onion into ½-inch thick slices and then break into rings.
3. Place pork rinds, coconut flour, beaten eggs, cream, and cheese into separate bowls.
4. Working on one onion ring at a time, first coat with coconut flour and dip into egg and cream and then cover with pork rinds and parmesan cheese.
5. When all the onion rings are coated in this manner, coat them again in the same manner and then place on a greased baking sheet.
6. Place the baking sheet into the oven and let bake for 15 minutes or until nicely golden brown.
7. Serve immediately.

Mug Bread

Servings: 1.
Preparation time: 10 minutes
Cooking time: 1 minutes
Total time: 11 minutes

Nutrition Value:
Calories: 275 Cal, Carbs: 3.2 g, Net Carbs: 2.3 g, Fat: 26.3 g, Protein: 8.3 g, Fiber: 0.9 g.

Ingredients:

- 4 tablespoons almond flour
- 1/8 teaspoon salt
- ½ teaspoon baking powder
- 1 tablespoon olive oil
- 1 egg

Method:

1. Place all the ingredients in a microwave ovenproof mug and stir until well mixed.
2. Place mug into the oven and let bake for 1 minute at high heat setting or until cooked thoroughly, inserted wooden toothpick into mug should come out clean.
3. When done, turn out bread and let cool slightly.
4. Then slice bread and serve.

CHAPTER 11: BEEF, PORK & LAMB

Lemon Garlic Pork Steaks

Servings: 4.

Preparation time: 10 minutes

Cooking time: 30 minutes

Total time: 40 minutes

Nutrition Value:

Calories: 483 Cal, Carbs: 6 g, Net Carbs: 5 g, Fat: 28 g, Protein: 50 g, Fiber: 1 g.

Ingredients:

- 4 large pork steaks
- 8-ounce cremini mushrooms, quartered
- 1 lemon, sliced
- 2 tablespoons chopped parsley
- 3 teaspoons minced garlic
- 2 teaspoons lemon pepper seasoning
- 1 1/2 teaspoon sea salt
- 3 tablespoons unsalted butter
- 3 tablespoons olive oil
- 1 cup chicken stock

Method:

1. Rinse pork steaks, pat dry and then season with salt and lemon pepper seasoning on all sides.
2. Heat a large skillet on medium-high heat and melt 2 tablespoons of each butter and olive oil.
3. Then add seasoned pork steams and let cook for 4 to 5 minutes per side or until cooked through.
4. When done, remove steaks from pan and add remaining butter and oil to pan along with ½ cup chicken stock.

5. Switch heat to medium level and deglaze the pan and scrape the bottom of the pan.
6. Add mushrooms and garlic and let cook for 3 minutes or until mushrooms are softened.
7. Pour in remaining chicken stock, add lemon slices and let simmer for 5 minutes.
8. Return pork steaks to pan and let cook for 8 to 10 minutes, flipping steaks frequently.
9. Serve when ready.

Stuffed Bacon Cheeseburger

Servings: 4 chicken breasts.
Preparation time: 10 minutes
Cooking time: 10 minutes
Total time: 20 minutes

Nutrition Value:
Calories: 613 Cal, Carbs: 1.5 g, Net Carbs: 1.5 g, Fat: 51 g, Protein: 33 g, Fiber: 0 g.

Ingredients:

- 8-ounce ground beef
- 2 slices of bacon, cooked
- 1 teaspoon salt
- 1/2 teaspoon ground black pepper
- 1 teaspoon Cajun seasoning
- 1 tablespoon unsalted butter
- 1-ounce mozzarella cheese, cubed
- 2-ounce cheddar cheese, sliced

Method:

1. Place beef in a large bowl and stir in salt, black pepper, and Cajun seasoning until mixed.
2. Shape mixture into two patties, then evenly divided mozzarella cheese cube in the middle of patties and enclose with beef.
3. Place a pan over medium heat, add butter and when melted, add a patty.
4. Cover pan and let cook for 3 minutes per side and then top with a cheddar cheese slice.
5. Return lid to the pan and continue cooking for 2 minutes.
6. Transfer patty to a plate and cook remaining patty in the same manner.
7. Top each patty with a bacon slice and serve.

Meatloaf

Servings: 6 slices.
Preparation time: 10 minutes
Cooking time: 1 hour
Total time: 1 hour and 10 minutes

Nutrition Value:
Calories: 377 Cal, Carbs: 5 g, Net Carbs: 4 g, Fat: 25 g, Protein: 32 g, Fiber: 1 g.

Ingredients:

- 32-ounce ground beef
- 1 ½ teaspoon minced garlic
- 1 teaspoon salt
- 1/2 teaspoon ground black pepper
- 1/4 teaspoon blackstrap molasses
- 1 1/2 teaspoons swerve sweetener
- 1 tablespoon red chili powder
- 1 teaspoon dried cilantro
- 1 tablespoon Worcestershire sauce
- 2 eggs
- 5-ounce cup tomato ketchup, organic and low carb
- 4 ounces shredded cheddar cheese

Method:

1. Set oven to 375 degrees F and let preheat.
2. Place beef in a bowl and add garlic, salt, black pepper, chili powder, cilantro, Worcestershire sauce, eggs, 1/3 cup ketchup, and cheese.
3. Stir until well mixed and spoon mixture into a loaf pan.
4. Stir together remaining ketchup, molasses and swerve sweetener until well combined and then generously brush this mixture all over the top of the meatloaf.

5. Place loaf pan into the oven and let bake for 50 to 60 minutes or until top is nicely browned and inserted meat thermometer reads 145 degrees F.
6. When done, take out meatloaf and let cool slightly on wire rack.
7. Slice to serve.

Pork Stroganoff

Servings: 4.
Preparation time: 10 minutes
Cooking time: 25 minutes
Total time: 35 minutes

Nutrition Value:
Calories: 250.5 Cal, Carbs: 12.1 g, Net Carbs: 10.6 g, Fat: 10 g, Protein: 27.6 g, Fiber: 1.3 g.

Ingredients:

- 16-ounce pork fillets, sliced into thin strips
- 8-ounce mushrooms, sliced
- 1 medium-sized white onion, peeled and diced
- 1 teaspoon sun-dried tomato paste
- 1 ½ teaspoon minced garlic
- 1 teaspoon salt
- 1 teaspoon ground black pepper
- 1 teaspoon red chili powder
- 1 tablespoon paprika
- 1 tablespoon mustard paste, organic
- 1 teaspoon lemon juice
- 1 tablespoon coconut oil
- 2 tablespoons crème Fraiche
- 7-ounce heavy cream

Method:

1. Place a large skillet over high heat, add oil and when heated, add onion and garlic.
2. Let cook for 5 minutes or until softened and then pork fillets.
3. Let cook for 8 to 10 minutes or until browned on all sides and cooked through and then add mushrooms.

4. Continue cooking for 3 to 4 minutes or until softened and then stir in crème Fraiche and cream until combined.
5. Stir in tomato paste, salt, black pepper, chili powder, paprika, mustard and lemon juice.
6. Let cook for 2 minutes and then serve.

Egg Roll in a Bowl

Servings: 6.
Preparation time: 10 minutes
Cooking time: 15 minutes
Total time: 25 minutes

Nutrition Value:
Calories: 268 Cal, Carbs: 10 g, Net Carbs: 6 g, Fat: 3 g, Protein: 15 g, Fiber: 4 g.

Ingredients:

- 16-ounce ground pork
- 1 head of cabbage, thinly sliced
- 2 sliced green onions, green parts only
- 1 small white onion, peeled and sliced
- 1 teaspoon grated ginger
- ½ teaspoon minced garlic
- 1 teaspoon salt
- ¾ teaspoon ground black pepper
- 1 tablespoon sesame oil
- ¼ cup soy sauce
- 2 tablespoons chicken broth

Method:

1. Place a large skillet pan over medium heat and when heated, add pork and heat for 7 to 10 minutes or until nicely browned.
2. Stir in onion and oil and continue cooking for 3 minutes or until onion softened.
3. Stir in ginger, garlic and soy sauce in a bowl and add this mixture to pan.
4. Stir to combine, add cabbage and toss to coat.
5. Stir in chicken broth and continue cooking for 3 minutes, stirring frequently.
6. Season with salt and black pepper and remove the pan from heat.
7. Garnish with green onions and serve.

Cheesesteak Casserole

Servings: 6.
Preparation time: 10 minutes
Cooking time: 20 minutes
Total time: 30 minutes

Nutrition Value:
Calories: 367.8 Cal, Carbs: 8.4 g, Net Carbs: 6.1 g, Fat: 24.9 g, Protein: 30.8 g, Fiber: 2.3 g.

Ingredients:

- 12-ounce beef steak, sliced
- 3 medium-sized green bell peppers, cored and sliced
- 8-ounce sliced mushrooms
- 3 medium-sized white onions, peeled and sliced
- 1 teaspoon minced garlic
- 1 teaspoon salt
- 1 tablespoon Italian seasoning
- ½ teaspoon crushed red pepper flakes
- 2 tablespoons coconut oil
- 6 slices of Swiss cheese

Method:

1. Set oven to 375 degrees F and let preheat.
2. In the meantime, place a large skillet over medium heat, add coconut oil and when melted, add all ingredients except for cheese.
3. Let cook for 5 minutes or until softened.
4. Then spoon mixture into a 9 by 13-inch baking pan and top with cheese.
5. Place baking pan into the oven and let bake for 15 minutes or until cheese melts.
6. Serve when ready.

Pepperoni Pizza

Servings: 1 pizza.
Preparation time: 10 minutes
Cooking time: 25 minutes
Total time: 35 minutes

Nutrition Value:
Calories: 1069 Cal, Carbs: 11 g, Net Carbs: 8 g, Fat: 90 g, Protein: 55 g, Fiber: 3 g.

Ingredients:

- 1½ ounce pepperoni slices
- 3 tablespoons sliced Olives
- 5-ounce leafy greens
- 1 teaspoon sea salt
- ¾ teaspoon ground black pepper
- 1 teaspoon dried oregano
- 3 tablespoons tomato paste
- 4 tablespoons olive oil
- 4 eggs
- 6-ounce shredded mozzarella cheese
- 5-ounce grated cheddar cheese

Method:

1. Set oven to 400 degrees F and let preheat.
2. To prepare crust, whisk together eggs and mozzarella cheese until combined and then spread this mixture on a pizza pan or baking sheet, lined with parchment paper.
3. Place pizza pan into the oven and let bake for 15 minutes or until top is nicely golden brown.
4. When done, remove the pan from oven and let cool for 2 minutes.

5. Spread tomato paste on top of the crust, then sprinkle with oregano and cheddar cheese and scatter with pepperoni slices.
6. Increase oven temperature to 450 degrees F, return pizza pan to the oven and let bake for 10 minutes or until cheese melt completely.
7. Slice to serve.

Lamb Curry

Servings: 6.
Preparation time: 10 minutes
Cooking time: 8 hours
Total time: 8 hours and 10 minutes

Nutrition Value:
Calories: 158 Cal, Carbs: 6.7 g, Net Carbs: 2.9 g, Fat: 7.1 g, Protein: 20.3 g, Fiber: 3.8 g, Salt: 654 mg, Cholesterol: 94 mg.

Ingredients:

- 18-ounce cubed lamb
- 18-ounces frozen spinach, thawed
- 14 ounce chopped tomatoes
- 1 medium-sized red onion, peeled and sliced
- 1 tablespoon minced garlic
- 2 tablespoons grated ginger
- 1/2 teaspoon red chili powder
- 1 teaspoon garam masala powder
- 2 teaspoons cumin powder
- 2 teaspoons ground coriander
- 1 teaspoon turmeric powder
- 2 teaspoons ground cardamom
- 6 whole cloves

Method:

1. Squeeze moisture from spinach and place in a 6-quart slow cooker.
2. Add remaining ingredients to the slow cooker and stir until mixed.
3. Cover slow cooker with its lid and let cook for 8 hours on low heat setting or for 5 hours on the high heat setting.
4. Serve when ready.

Pork & Noodle Stir Fry

Servings: 4.
Preparation time: 10 minutes
Cooking time: 15 minutes 1 hour
Total time: 25 minutes

Nutrition Value:
Calories: 343 Cal, Carbs: 10 g, Net Carbs: 6 g, Fat: 21 g, Protein: 28 g, Fiber: 4 g.

Ingredients:

- 16-ounce pork sirloin, fat trimmed and thinly sliced
- 4 tablespoons coconut flour, divided
- 2 cups miracle noodles
- 3 cups chopped white cabbage
- 1 cup sliced red bell pepper
- 1/2 cup green onions, sliced
- 2 tablespoons minced ginger
- 1 teaspoon minced garlic
- ½ teaspoon salt
- 2 tablespoons erythritol sweetener
- ½ teaspoon cayenne pepper
- 1 tablespoon sesame seeds, toasted
- 1 tablespoon lime juice
- ¼ cup olive oil
- 1 teaspoon sesame oil
- 3 tablespoons soy sauce
- 1 tablespoon fish sauce
- 1/2 cup water

Method:

1. Place pork in a bowl, add flour, salt, and pepper and toss to coat.

2. Place a skillet pan over medium-high heat, add olive and sesame oil and when heated, add coated pork pieces.
3. Let cook for 4 minutes or until crispy and cooked through.
4. When done, transfer pork to a plate and add peppers, cabbage, ginger, and garlic.
5. Let cook for 2 minutes or until cabbage wilts.
6. In the meantime, whisk together soy sauce, fish sauce, and erythritol sweetener until combined and then add this sauce to the pan along with noodles.
7. Continue cooking for 4 minutes or until sauce starts bubbling and reduced by half.
8. Remove pan from heat, drizzle with lemon juice, garnish with green onion and sesame seeds.
9. Serve straightaway.

Coffee-Chipotle Pork Chops

Servings: 4.
Preparation time: 10 minutes plus marinating time
Cooking time: 45 minutes
Total time: 55 minutes

Nutrition Value:
Calories: 234.7 Cal, Carbs: 4.6 g, Net Carbs: 4.5 g, Fat: 7.2 g, Protein: 34.6 g, Fiber: 0.1 g.

Ingredients:

- 4 bone-in pork chops
- 2½ tablespoons lard
- ½ teaspoon garlic powder
- 1 tablespoon ground coffee, dark roasted
- 1 tablespoon sea salt
- ½ tablespoon ground black pepper
- ½ teaspoon chipotle chili powder
- 1½ teaspoons coconut sugar
- ½ teaspoon ground allspice
- ½ teaspoon ground cinnamon
- ½ teaspoon ground cumin

Method:

1. Place all the ingredients except for pork chops and lard in a bowl and stir until mixed
2. Rub this spice rub all over pork chops until well coated and then place pork chops in a large resealable bag.
3. Seal the bag and let pork chops marinate in refrigerate for 8 hours.
4. Then let thaw them at room temperature for 30 minutes before cooking.
5. Set oven to 350 degrees F and let preheat.

6. Place a large skillet pan over medium heat, add lard and when heated, add marinated pork chops.
7. Let pork chops sear for 3 minutes per side and then transfer pan into the oven.
8. Let bake for 10 minutes or until meat thermometer inserted into thickest part of chops read 145 degrees F.
9. When done, let pork chops rest for 10 minutes before serving.

Pecan Crusted Rack of Lamb

Servings: 3.
Preparation time: 10 minutes
Cooking time: 50 minutes
Total time: 60 minutes

Nutrition Value:
Calories: 369.6 Cal, Carbs: 4.6 g, Net Carbs: 3.5 g, Fat: 22.2 g, Protein: 33.3 g, Fiber: 1.1 g.

Ingredients:

- 1 rack of lamb, grass-fed
- ¼ cup chopped white onion
- 1 ½ teaspoon minced garlic
- 1 teaspoon salt
- ¾ teaspoon ground black pepper
- 1 tablespoon mustard paste, organic
- 1 cup pecans, grounded
- 1 lime, zested
- 2 tablespoons unsalted butter

Method:

1. Set oven to 400 degrees F and let preheat.
2. Trim fat from a rack of lamb and then rub with salt and black pepper.
3. Place rack of lamb on a roasting tray and then bake for 10 minutes.
4. In the meantime, place a frying pan over medium heat, add butter and when melted, add onions.
5. Let cook for 3 to 5 minutes or until softened and then stir in garlic, lime zest, and pecans.
6. Let cook for 2 minutes and then remove the pan from heat.
7. Let rack of lamb cool slightly, then coat with mustard and prepared pecan mixture.
8. Return rack of lamb on a roasting tray and continue to bake for 25 to 30 minutes or until meat thermometer inserted into lamb reads 145 degrees F.

9. When done, let rack of lamb rest for 10 minutes.
10. Slice to serve.

Lamb Slider Patties

Servings: 8.
Preparation time: 15 minutes
Cooking time: 10 minutes
Total time: 25 minutes

Nutrition Value:
Calories: 145.9 Cal, Carbs: 1.9 g, Net Carbs: 1.3 g, Fat: 11 g, Protein: 9.4 g, Fiber: 0.6 g.

Ingredients:

- 16-ounce ground lamb
- ½ of a medium-sized white onion, minced
- 1 ½ teaspoon minced garlic
- 1 tablespoon dried dill
- 1 teaspoon salt
- ½ teaspoon ground black pepper

Method:

1. Place all the ingredients in a large bowl and stir until well combined.
2. Then shape mixture into 8 patties.
3. Preheat grill over medium heat and then place patties on it.
4. Let grill for 5 minutes per side or until cooked through.
5. Serve with your favorite low-carb dip as a lettuce wrap.

CHAPTER 12: POULTRY

Chicken Carbonara

Servings: 4.
Preparation time: 15 minutes
Cooking time: 20 minutes
Total time: 35 minutes

Nutrition Value:
Calories: 860 Cal, Carbs: 11 g, Net Carbs: 9 g, Fat: 80 g, Protein: 25 g, Fiber: 2 g.

Ingredients:

- 10-ounce bacon, diced
- 30-ounce zucchini
- 2 tablespoons chopped parsley
- 1 teaspoon salt
- ¾ teaspoon ground black pepper
- 1 tablespoon unsalted butter
- 1¼ cups heavy whipping cream
- ¼ cup sour cream
- 3-ounce grated parmesan cheese
- 4 egg yolks

Method:

1. Place a skillet pan over medium heat and when heated, add bacon and let cook for 4 to 5 minutes or until crispy.
2. Place a saucepan over medium heat, add cream and bring to boil.
3. Then reduce heat to low and continue boiling for 3 to 5 minutes or until cream is reduced by fourth.
4. Remove saucepan when done and whisk in salt, black pepper, and sour cream until combined.
5. Return saucepan to heat and let cook for 3 minutes or until warm through.

6. When done, remove the pan from heat.
7. Trim zucchini and then spiralize into noodles, spaghetti-sized, using a spiralizer.
8. Add zucchini noodles into the cream sauce and then divide this mixture evenly into four proportions.
9. Evenly top each with crispy bacon, an egg yolk and sprinkle with parsley and cheese.
10. Serve immediately.

Chicken Caesar Salad

Servings: 2.
Preparation time: 15 minutes
Cooking time: 20 minutes
Total time: 35 minutes

Nutrition Value:
Calories: 1191 Cal, Carbs: 9 g, Net Carbs: 5 g, Fat: 102 g, Protein: 57 g, Fiber: 4 g.

Ingredients:

- 10-ounce chicken breasts
- 2 tablespoons chopped anchovies filets
- 5 1/3-ounce bacon
- ½ of a lettuce
- 1 tablespoon olive oil
- 1 ½ teaspoon salt, divided
- 1 ¼ teaspoon ground black pepper, divided
- 1 tablespoon mustard paste, organic
- ½ of a lemon, zest, and juice
- ¾ cup grated parmesan cheese, divided
- ½ cup mayonnaise, organic

Method:

1. Set oven to 400 degrees F and let preheat.
2. Prepare the dressing by placing anchovies in a blender, along with mustard, cheese, ½ teaspoon salt, ½ teaspoon black pepper, lemon juice, lemon zest and 2 tablespoons parmesan cheese.
3. Pulse at high speed until smooth, then tip dressing in a bowl and let chill in refrigerator until required.
4. Take a baking dish, grease with non-stick cooking spray and place chicken breasts in it.

5. Season with remaining salt and black pepper, then drizzle with olive oil.
6. Place baking dish into the oven and let bake for 20 minutes or until top is nicely golden brown and cooked through.
7. In the meantime, place a skillet pan over medium-high heat, when heated add Bacon and let cook for 5 minutes or until crispy.
8. When done, remove bacon from the pan and dice.
9. Shred lettuce and evenly divide into two serving platters.
10. Top with baked chicken and then scatter with bacon.
11. Drizzle with a dressing generously, sprinkle with remaining cheese and serve.

Turkey Sausage Frittata

Servings: 8 slices.
Preparation time: 15 minutes
Cooking time: 40 minutes
Total time: 55 minutes

Nutrition Value:
Calories: 240 Cal, Carbs: 5.5 g, Net Carbs: 3.1 g, Fat: 16.7 g, Protein: 17.3 g, Fiber: 2.4 g.

Ingredients:

- 12-ounce ground turkey breakfast sausage
- 2 green bell peppers, cored
- 1 teaspoon salt
- 1 teaspoon ground black pepper
- 2 teaspoons unsalted butter
- 1 cup sour cream
- 12 eggs

Method:

1. Set oven to 350 degrees F and let preheat.
2. In the meantime, place salt, black pepper, cream in a blender.
3. Crack eggs in it and then blend at high speed until smooth.
4. Tip mixture into a bowl and set aside until required.
5. Place a large skillet over medium heat, when heated add butter and let melt.
6. Cut peppers into thin strips, add to pan and let cook for 6 minutes or until nicely golden brown.
7. When done, transfer to a plate and add sausage to pan.
8. Let cook for 8 to 10 minutes or until nicely golden brown, stirring frequently.
9. When done, spread sausage all over the pan and then scatter with pepper.
10. Spread with prepared egg mixture and then place pan into the oven.
11. Let bake for 30 minutes until top is nicely golden brown and frittata is cooked through.

12. Slice to serve.

White Turkey Chili

Servings: 5.
Preparation time: 10 minutes
Cooking time: 20 minutes
Total time: 30 minutes

Nutrition Value:
Calories: 388 Cal, Carbs: 5.5 g, Net Carbs: 4.8 g, Fat: 30.5 g, Protein: 28.8 g, Fiber: 0.7 g.

Ingredients:

- 16-ounce ground turkey
- 2 cups riced cauliflower
- 1 medium-sized white onion, minced
- 1 ½ teaspoon minced garlic
- 1 teaspoon garlic powder
- 1 teaspoon celery salt
- 1 teaspoon salt
- 1 teaspoon black pepper
- 1 teaspoon thyme
- 1 tablespoon mustard paste, organic
- 2 tablespoons coconut oil
- 2 cups coconut milk, unsweetened
- ½ cup grated cheddar cheese

Method:

1. Place a large pot over medium heat, add oil and when heated, add onion and garlic and let cook for 3 minutes.
2. Then add turkey and riced cauliflower and stir in garlic powder, celery salt, salt, black pepper, thyme, and mustard until well combined.
3. Let cook for 5 to 7 minutes or until meat is nicely browned.
4. Then pour in coconut milk and let simmer for 8 to 10 minutes, stirring frequently.

5. Divide chili evenly among serving bowl, garnish with cheese and serve.

Mushroom Chicken

Servings: 2.
Preparation time: 10 minutes
Cooking time: 20 minutes
Total time: 30 minutes

Nutrition Value:
Calories: 334 Cal, Carbs: 3.2 g, Net Carbs: 1.1 g, Fat: 27.3 g, Protein: 24.3 g, Fiber: 2.1 g.

Ingredients:

- 2 chicken cutlets
- 5 cremini mushrooms, sliced
- 1 small white onion, peeled and sliced
- ½ teaspoon salt
- ½ teaspoon dried thyme
- 3 tablespoons unsalted butter
- 1/3 cup coconut milk, unsweetened

Method:

1. Place a large skillet over medium heat and when hot, add 2 tablespoons butter.
2. Let butter melt, add mushrooms and season with ¼ teaspoon salt.
3. Let cook for 3 to 5 minutes or until nicely golden brown and then add onions.
4. Let cook for 6 minutes or until tender and then transfer mushroom-onion mixture to a plate.
5. Add remaining butter to the pan and let melt.
6. Season chicken with salt and thyme and add to pan.
7. Let cook for 5 minutes per side or until meat is no longer pink.
8. Return mushroom mixture to pan and pour in coconut milk.
9. Let simmer for 2 minutes or until heated through and then serve.

Fried Chicken

Servings: 8.
Preparation time: 10 minutes
Cooking time: 30 minutes
Total time: 40 minutes

Nutrition Value:
Calories: 463 Cal, Carbs: 7 g, Net Carbs: 4 g, Fat: 15 g, Protein: 33 g, Fiber: 3 g.

Ingredients:

- 8 chicken thighs
- 1 teaspoon salt
- 1 teaspoon ground black pepper
- 1 teaspoon dried parsley
- 1/2 cup sesame seeds
- 1 cup sunflower seeds
- 2 tablespoons avocado oil

Method:

1. Set oven to 425 degrees F and let preheat.
2. Place a rimmed baking sheet, grease with avocado oil and set aside until required.
3. Place sunflower and sesame seeds in a blender along with salt, black pepper and parsley and pulse until mixture resembles crumbs.
4. Transfer this mixture in a large re-sealable freezer proof bag, add one chicken thigh and seal the bag.
5. Turn bag upside down until chicken is well coated with seed mixture and then place it onto the prepared baking sheet.
6. Coat remaining chicken thighs, one at a time, and place onto baking sheet.
7. Place the baking sheet into the oven and let bake for 30 minutes or until cooked through, flipping halfway through.
8. Serve straightaway.

Paprika Chicken

Servings: 4.
Preparation time: 10 minutes
Cooking time: 45 minutes
Total time: 55 minutes

Nutrition Value:
Calories: 669 Cal, Carbs: 6.1 g, Net Carbs: 4.4 g, Fat: 60.7 g, Protein: 23.7 g, Fiber: 1.7 g

Ingredients:

- 12 chicken drumsticks
- 4-ounce white onion, peeled and diced
- 4-ounce red pepper, cored and sliced
- ½ teaspoon salt
- ½ teaspoon ground black pepper
- 1 tablespoon paprika
- 2 tablespoons unsalted butter
- ¼ cup soured cream
- ¼ cup coconut milk, unsweetened
- 1 cup chicken broth

Method:

1. Rinse chicken, pat dry and season with salt and black pepper.
2. Place a large pot over medium heat, add 1 tablespoon butter and when melted, add seasoned chicken.
3. Increase heat medium-high and let cook for 5 to 7 minutes or until nicely golden brown on all sides.
4. Switch heat to low, then pour in chicken broth and let simmer for 30 minutes.
5. In the meantime, prepare onion and peppers.
6. Place a skillet pan over medium heat, add remaining butter and when melted, add onion.

7. Let cook for 3 to 5 minutes or until nicely golden brown.
8. Then add peppers and continue cooking for 5 minutes.
9. When done, remove the pan from heat and set aside until required.
10. When done, transfer chicken to a bowl and separate chicken meat from its bone and discard bones.
11. Shred chicken and set aside.
12. Add onion-pepper mixture, stir in paprika and blend mixture using an immersion blender until smooth.
13. Return pot to heat, stir in cream and return chicken to pot.
14. Let cook for 5 minutes and then serve.

Chicken Tenders

Servings: 2.
Preparation time: 10 minutes
Cooking time: 25 minutes
Total time: 35 minutes

Nutrition Value:
Calories: 587 Cal, Carbs: 12 g, Net Carbs: 4 g, Fat: 32 g, Protein: 63 g, Fiber: 8 g.

Ingredients:

- 8 chicken tenderloin
- ½ cup almond flour
- ¼ cup flaxseed meal
- ¼ teaspoon paprika
- 1 teaspoon salt
- ¾ teaspoon ground black pepper
- 2 eggs

Method:

1. Set oven to 375 degrees F and let preheat.
2. Take a large baking sheet, line with parchment sheet and set aside until required.
3. Place almond flour in a bowl and stir in remaining ingredients except for eggs.
4. Crack eggs in another bowl and whisk slightly.
5. Working on one chicken piece at a time, first dip chicken into egg, then coat with flour mixture evenly on all sides and place onto the prepared baking sheet.
6. Prepare remaining chicken pieces in the same manner and then place baking sheet into the oven.
7. Let bake for 25 minutes or until chicken is nicely golden brown and cooked through.
8. Serve with favorite low-carb sauce.

Jerk Chicken

Servings: 4.
Preparation time: 10 minutes plus marinating time
Cooking time: 30 minutes
Total time: 40 minutes

Nutrition Value:
Calories: 183.8 Cal, Carbs: 2.4 g, Net Carbs: 1.8 g, Fat: 4.7 g, Protein: 31.2 g, Fiber: 0.6 g.

Ingredients:

- 24-ounce chicken drumsticks and thighs
- 4 green onions, thinly sliced
- 2 teaspoons minced garlic
- 1 tablespoon grated ginger
- ½ teaspoon ground black pepper
- 1 teaspoon ground allspice
- ½ teaspoon ground cinnamon
- ¼ teaspoon ground nutmeg
- ¼ cup lime juice
- 1/3 cup soy sauce
- 1 tablespoon olive oil

Method:

1. Place all the ingredients except for chicken and green onions in a large bowl and whisk until well combined.
2. Then add chicken pieces and toss to coat.
3. Place bowl into the refrigerator and let marinate for 30 minutes or overnight.
4. When ready to cook, set grill and let preheat at high heat setting.
5. Remove chicken from marinade, place on grilling rack and let cook for 20 to 30 minutes or until cooked through.
6. Serve with green onions.

Lemon Chicken

Servings: 2.
Preparation time: 10 minutes
Cooking time: 20 minutes
Total time: 30 minutes

Nutrition Value:
Calories: 345 Cal, Carbs: 8.5 g, Net Carbs: 3.5 g, Fat: 25.5 g, Protein: 27.5 g, Fiber: 5 g.

Ingredients:

- 8-ounce chicken thighs
- 6 tablespoons coconut flour
- 1/4 teaspoon xanthan gum
- 2 tablespoons swerve sweetener
- 1 teaspoon lemon zest
- 4 tablespoons lemon juice
- 4 tablespoons coconut oil
- 1/2 cup chicken broth

Method:

1. Cut chicken pieces into bite-size pieces and set aside.
2. Place coconut flour in a bowl, add chicken pieces and toss until well coated.
3. Place a pan over medium-high heat, add oil and when heated, add coated chicken into a single layer.
4. Let cook for 7 to 10 minutes or until cooked through.
5. When done, transfer chicken to a plate and cook remaining chicken in the same manner.
6. While chicken cook, place a saucepan over high heat, add lemon zest and pour in broth.
7. Stir in sweetener until dissolves and then stir in xanthan gum and lemon juice.
8. Bring the mixture to boil, then reduce heat to low and let simmer until sauce reduces to desired thickness.

9. When chicken pieces are cooked, add to prepared lemon sauce and toss to coat.
10. Serve immediately.

CHAPTER 13: SEAFOOD

Salmon Steaks

Servings: 2.
Preparation time: 10 minutes plus marinating time
Cooking time: 20 minutes
Total time: 30 minutes

Nutrition Value:
Calories: 422.6 Cal, Carbs: 3.4 g, Net Carbs: 5.35 g, Fat: 36.5 g, Protein: 20.8 g, Fiber: 0.1 g.

Ingredients:

- 2 salmon steaks
- 2 teaspoons seasoning salt
- 1 teaspoon ground black pepper
- 1/4 cup unsalted butter, melted
- 1 teaspoon Worcestershire sauce
- 1/3 cup lemon juice

Method:

1. Set oven to 400 degrees F and let preheat.
2. In a bowl place all the ingredients except for salmon and whisk until combined.
3. Add salmon steaks and turn to coat.
4. Cover bowl and let marinate in the refrigerator for 30 minutes.
5. Then transfer marinated salmon to a baking pan and let bake for 20 minutes or until cooked through, flipping halfway through.
6. Transfer salmon steaks to a serving plate, drizzle with its sauce and serve.

Avocado Tuna Salad

Servings: 2.
Preparation time: 10 minutes
Cooking time: 0 minutes
Total time: 10 minutes

Nutrition Value:
Calories: 211 Cal, Carbs: 5 g, Net Carbs: 1.5 g, Fat: 16 g, Protein: 14 g, Fiber: 3.5 g.

Ingredients:

- 10-ounce cooked tuna
- 1 large avocado, peeled and cored
- 1 celery, chopped
- 1 teaspoon chopped parsley
- 2 tablespoons minced red onion
- 1 ½ teaspoon minced garlic
- 1 teaspoon salt
- ¾ teaspoon ground black pepper
- 2 teaspoon mustard paste, organic
- 3 tablespoons mayonnaise

Method:

1. Cut avocado into cubes and place in a large bowl.
2. Add remaining ingredients and stir until well mixed.
3. Serve immediately.

Cheesy Salmon with Broccoli

Servings: 4.
Preparation time: 10 minutes
Cooking time: 25 minutes
Total time: 35 minutes

Nutrition Value:
Calories: 713 Cal, Carbs: 9 g, Net Carbs: 6 g, Fat: 55 g, Protein: 46 g, Fiber: 3 g.

Ingredients:

- 24-ounce salmon fillets
- 14-ounce broccoli, cut into florets
- 1 ¼ teaspoon salt
- ¾ teaspoon ground black pepper
- 1 lime
- 4 ounce grated unsalted butter
- 6-ounce grated cheddar cheese

Method:

1. Set oven to 400 degrees F and let preheat.
2. Place broccoli florets in a saucepan, cover with water and let simmer for 10 minutes over medium-high heat or until tender.
3. Then drain broccoli and transfer to a baking dish, greased with non-stick cooking spray.
4. Sprinkle black pepper, butter, and cheese on top and place baking dish into the oven.
5. Let bake for 15 to 20 minutes or until cheese melt completely and the top is nicely golden brown.
6. In the meantime, place a frying pan over medium heat, add 4 tablespoons butter and when melted, add salmon in a single layer.
7. Cook for 5 minutes per side until cooked through and crispy.
8. When done, serve cheesy broccoli with salmon.

Shrimps & Artichoke

Servings: 2.
Preparation time: 15 minutes
Cooking time: 0 minutes
Total time: 15 minutes

Nutrition Value:
Calories: 928 Cal, Carbs: 14 g, Net Carbs: 7 g, Fat: 80 g, Protein: 36 g, Fiber: 7 g.

Ingredients:

- 10-ounce shrimps, peeled and cooked
- 14-ounce cooked artichokes
- 2-ounce baby spinach
- 6 sun-dried tomatoes in oil
- ¾ teaspoon salt
- ½ teaspoon ground black pepper
- 4 tablespoons olive oil
- ½ cup sour cream
- 4 eggs, hard-boiled

Method:

1. Peel boiled eggs, then cut evenly into slices and place in a plate.
2. Add shrimps, artichokes, tomatoes, and spinach to the plate.
3. Drizzle with sour cream and olive oil and season with salt and black pepper.
4. Toss to coat and serve.

Fish Casserole

Servings: 4.
Preparation time: 10 minutes
Cooking time: 30 minutes
Total time: 40 minutes

Nutrition Value:
Calories: 822 Cal, Carbs: 13 g, Net Carbs: 8 g, Fat: 69 g, Protein: 41 g, Fiber: 5 g.

Ingredients:

- 25-ounce white fish
- 2 tablespoons small capers
- 15-ounce broccoli, cut into florets
- 6 scallions, chopped
- 1 teaspoon salt
- ¼ teaspoon ground black pepper
- 1 tablespoon dried parsley
- 1 tablespoon mustard paste, organic
- 3-ounce unsalted butter, sliced
- 2 tablespoons olive oil
- 1¼ cups heavy whipping cream

Method:

1. Set oven to 400 degrees F and let preheat.
2. Place a frying pan over medium-high heat, add oil and when heated, add broccoli florets.
3. Let cook for 5 minutes or until nicely golden brown and tender.
4. Then season with salt and black pepper and add capers and scallion and continue frying for 2 minutes.
5. Spoon this mixture into a baking dish, greased with non-stick cooking spray and then create a well in the middle.

6. Add fish into the well and press vegetables in such a way that fish is nestled among the vegetables.
7. Whisk parsley, mustard, and cream in a bowl and pour this mixture over fish and vegetables.
8. Scatter slices of butter on top and place baking dish into the oven.
9. Let bake for 20 minutes or until vegetables and fish is cooked through.
10. Serve immediately

Clams Italiano

Servings: 2.
Preparation time: 10 minutes
Cooking time: 15 minutes
Total time: 25 minutes

Nutrition Value:
Calories: 227 Cal, Carbs: 4.4 g, Net Carbs: 3.8 g, Fat: 15.7 g, Protein: 5.2 g, Fiber: 0.6 g.

Ingredients:

- 36 clams in shell, scrubbed
- 2 ½ teaspoons minced garlic
- 1 teaspoon salt
- ¾ teaspoon ground black pepper
- 1 teaspoon crushed red pepper flakes
- 1 tablespoon dried oregano
- 1 tablespoon dried parsley
- 4-ounce unsalted butter
- 2 cups dry white wine

Method:

1. Place a skillet pan over medium heat, add butter and when melted, add garlic.
2. Let cook for 2 to 3 minutes or until fragrant.
3. Then add remaining ingredients except for clams and stir until combined.
4. Add clams and stir until well coated.
5. Let cook for 5 to 7 minutes or until clams are opened, covering the pan.
6. Remove unopened clams from pan and discard them.
7. Ladle remaining clams into bowls and serve.

Thai fish & Coconut Curry

Servings: 4.
Preparation time: 10 minutes
Cooking time: 20 minutes
Total time: 30 minutes

Nutrition Value:
Calories: 880 Cal, Carbs: 14 g, Net Carbs: 9 g, Fat: 75 g, Protein: 42 g, Fiber: 4 g.

Ingredients:

- 2 tablespoons olive oil
- 25-ounce salmon fillets
- 1 ½ teaspoon salt
- 1 teaspoon ground black pepper
- 4 tablespoons unsalted butter, chopped
- 2 tablespoons red curry paste
- 14-ounce coconut cream
- 25 teaspoon cilantros, chopped
- 15-ounce cauliflower head, cut into florets

Method:

1. Set oven to 400 degrees F and let preheat.
2. Cut salmon into bite-sized pieces.
3. In the meantime, take a medium-sized baking dish, then grease with olive oil and place salmon fillets in it.
4. Season with salt and black pepper and then scatter with butter pieces.
5. Whisk together cilantro, curry paste and coconut cream until combined and then evenly pour this mixture over salmon.
6. Place baking dish into the oven and let bake for 20 minutes or until cooked through.
7. In the meantime, place cauliflower florets in a saucepan, cover with water, stir in salt and bring to boil and cook until tender.

8. Drain cauliflower florets and serve with salmon.

Jalapeno Shrimp Veggies Bake

Servings: 4.
Preparation time: 10 minutes
Cooking time: 45 minutes
Total time: 55 minutes

Nutrition Value:
Calories: 194 Cal, Carbs: 2 g, Net Carbs: 5.35 g, Fat: 3 g, Protein: 34 g, Fiber: 0 g, Salt: 654 mg, Cholesterol: 94 mg.

Ingredients:

- 10 medium-sized shrimps, peeled
- 2 zucchinis
- 1 large tomato
- ¼ cup chopped cilantro
- 1 jalapeño pepper
- 1/4 cup sliced red onion
- 1 teaspoon minced garlic
- 1 teaspoon sea salt
- ¾ teaspoon ground black pepper
- 1/2 teaspoon chili pepper flakes
- ¼ cup almond flour
- 2 tablespoons unsalted butter, melted
- 1/3 cup sour cream
- 2 eggs
- 1/2 cup grated parmesan cheese

Method:

1. Set oven to 350 degrees F and let preheat.
2. Cut zucchini into ¼ inch thick slices, cut tomatoes into 1/3-inch-thick slices and sliced jalapeno peppers.

3. Layer zucchini, tomato, pepper and onion slices in a baking dish and then top with shrimps.
4. In a bowl stir together garlic, flour, butter, cream, and eggs until smooth and then pour this mixture evenly over shrimps and vegetables.
5. Season with salt, black pepper, and then sprinkle with cheese and red pepper flakes.
6. Place baking dish into the oven and let bake for 45 minutes or until cheese is completely and shrimps are cooked through.
7. Serve immediately.

CHAPTER 14: SOUPS & SIDES

No-Noodle Chicken Soup

Servings: 8 bowls.
Preparation time: 10 minutes
Cooking time: 20 minutes
Total time: 1 hour and 45 minutes

Nutrition Value:
Calories: 509 Cal, Carbs: 4 g, Net Carbs: 4 g, Fat: 3 g, Protein: 33 g, Fiber: 1 g.

Ingredients:

- 1 ½ cooked shredded chickens
- 2 stalks of celery
- 6-ounce sliced mushrooms
- 2 cups green cabbage, cut into strips
- 1 medium-sized carrot, peeled and diced
- 2 tablespoons minced onion
- 1 ½ teaspoons minced garlic
- 1 teaspoon salt
- ¼ teaspoon ground black pepper
- 2 teaspoons dried parsley
- 4-ounce unsalted butter
- 8 cups chicken broth

Method:

1. Place a large pot over medium heat, add butter and let heat until melt.
2. Then add celery, mushrooms, onion, and garlic and let cook for four minutes or until fragrant and nicely golden brown.
3. Add carrots, then stir in salt, black pepper and parsley and pour in broth.
4. Stir until well mixed and then simmer for 15 to 20 minutes or until vegetables are tender.

5. Stir in chicken and cabbage into the soup and continue simmering for 10 to 12 minutes or until cabbage is tender.
6. When done, ladle soup into bowls and serve.

Avocado & Egg Salad

Servings: 4 plates.
Preparation time: 15 minutes
Cooking time: 0 minutes
Total time: 15 minutes

Nutrition Value:
Calories: 436 Cal, Carbs: 13.7 g, Net Carbs: 6.1 g, Fat: 36.3 g, Protein: 17 g, Fiber: 7.6 g.

Ingredients:

- 7-ounce avocado, peeled and cored
- 2 cups lettuce leaves
- 2 cups arugula
- 1 ½ teaspoon minced garlic
- ¾ teaspoon salt
- ½ teaspoon ground black pepper
- 2 teaspoons mustard paste, organic
- ½ cup soured cream
- 4 boiled eggs, organic

Method:

1. In a bowl, stir together garlic, salt, black pepper, mustard and sour cream until combined.
2. Rinse lettuce and arugula, then dry completely in a salad spinner and place in a large bowl.
3. Add prepared sour cream dressing and toss to coat.
4. Slice avocado and place on salad.
5. Peel eggs, then cut each egg evenly into four pieces and top on a salad.
6. Serve salad straight away.

Mackerel Salad

Servings: 2 plates.
Preparation time: 15 minutes
Cooking time: 10 minutes
Total time: 25 minutes

Nutrition Value:
Calories: 609 Cal, Carbs: 16.1 g, Net Carbs: 7.6 g, Fat: 49.9 g, Protein: 27.3 34 g, Fiber: 8.5 g.

Ingredients:

- 6.3-ounce mackerel fillets
- 5.3-ounce avocado
- 7.1-ounce green beans
- 2 cups lettuce leaves
- 2 cups arugula
- 1/2 teaspoon salt, divided
- 1/4 teaspoon ground black pepper
- 1 teaspoon mustard paste, organic
- 2 tablespoons lemon juice
- 1 tablespoon melted coconut oil
- 2 tablespoons olive oil
- 2 boiled eggs, organic

Method:

1. Fill a small sauce half full of water, add ¼ teaspoon salt, then add green beans and bring to boil over medium heat.
2. Let boil for 5 minutes or until beans are tender crisp.
3. When done, drain beans and set aside until required.
4. On each mackerel fillet, make small size diagonal cuts and then season with salt and black pepper on all sides.

5. Place a skillet pan over medium-high heat, add coconut oil and when heated, add the fillet, skin-side down.
6. Let cook for 4 to 5 minutes per side or until meat is no longer pink and cooked through.
7. When done, transfer fillets to a plate lined with paper towel and set aside.
8. Rinse lettuce and arugula, then dry completely in a salad spinner and place in a large bowl.
9. Peel eggs, cut each egg into four pieces and add to salad bowl along with mackerel slices.
10. Whisk together mustard, lemon juice, and olive oil until incorporated and then drizzle this dressing all over the salad.
11. Serve immediately.

Zuppa Toscana Soup

Servings: 10 bowls.
Preparation time: 10 minutes
Cooking time: 4 hours and 10 minutes
Total time: 4 hours and 20 minutes

Nutrition Value:
Calories: 246 Cal, Carbs: 7 g, Net Carbs: 5.7 g, Fat: 3 g, Protein: 14 g, Fiber: 1.3 g.

Ingredients:

- 12-ounce ground Italian sausage
- 1 large cauliflower head, cut into small florets
- 3 cups chopped kale
- ½ cup diced white onion
- 2 teaspoons minced garlic
- 1 teaspoon salt
- ½ teaspoon ground black pepper
- ¼ teaspoon crushed red pepper flakes
- 1 tablespoon olive oil
- ½ cup heavy cream
- 36 ounces vegetable stock

Method:

1. Place skillet pan over medium heat and when heated, add sausage.
2. Let cook for 5 to 7 minutes or until nicely golden brown.
3. When done, spoon meat into a 6-quart slow cooker.
4. Return pan to heat, add oil and onion and let cook for 4 minutes or until softened.
5. Spoon onion into the slow cooker along with remaining ingredients and stir until well combined.
6. Cover slow cooker with its lid, plug in and let cook for 4 hours at high heat setting or 8 hours at low heat setting.

7. When done, stir in cream and then ladle soup into serving bowls.
8. Serve straight away.

Mexican Chicken Soup

Servings: 4 bowls.
Preparation time: 10 minutes
Cooking time: 3 hours and 40 minutes
Total time: 3 hours and 50 minutes

Nutrition Value:
Calories: 194 Cal, Carbs: 2 g, Net Carbs: 5.35 g, Fat: 3 g, Protein: 34 g, Fiber: 0 g.

Ingredients:

- 14-ounce chicken breast
- 10-ounce tomatoes, fire-roasted
- 1 medium-sized red bell pepper
- ¼ cup chopped cilantro
- 1 medium-sized white onion, peeled and diced
- 1 tablespoon minced garlic
- 1 teaspoon salt
- 1 ½ teaspoon chipotle chili powder
- 1 teaspoon paprika
- 1 teaspoon Mexican seasoning
- 1 teaspoon cumin powder
- 1 teaspoon dried oregano
- 1 cup heavy cream
- 1/2 cup cream cheese
- 1 cup shredded cheddar cheese
- 1 ½ cups chicken stock

Method:

1. Place a skillet pan over medium heat, add oil and when heated, add onion and garlic.
2. Let cook for 4 to 5 minutes or until nicely golden brown.

3. In the meantime, place chicken breasts in a 6-quart slow cooker and top with tomatoes.
4. Spoon in cooked onion mixture and season with salt, chili powder, paprika, Mexican seasoning, cumin powder, and oregano.
5. Pour in chicken stock and then cover slow cooker with its lid.
6. Let cook for 3 hours at high heat setting.
7. When done, transfer chicken breast to a cutting board and shred using forks.
8. Return shredded chicken to slow cooker and stir until mixed.
9. Stir in pepper, cream, and cheeses.
10. Cover slow cooker with its lid and continue cooking for 30 minutes at high heat setting.
11. When done, ladle soup into serving bowls, then garnish with cilantro and serve.

Beef Stroganoff Soup

Servings: 6 bowls.
Preparation time: 10 minutes
Cooking time: 20 minutes
Total time: 30 minutes

Nutrition Value:
Calories: 520 Cal, Carbs: 9.8 g, Net Carbs: 8.4 g, Fat: 38.4 g, Protein: 34.9 g, Fiber: 1.4 g.

Ingredients:

- 2 large beef sirloin steaks, thinly sliced
- 21-ounce white mushrooms, cored and sliced
- 1/4 cup chopped parsley
- 4-ounce white onion, peeled and chopped
- 1 ½ teaspoon minced garlic
- 1 teaspoon salt
- 1/4 teaspoon ground black pepper
- 2 teaspoons paprika
- 1 tablespoon mustard paste, organic
- 1/4 cup unsalted butter
- 4 tablespoons lemon juice
- 1 1/2 cup sour cream
- 5 cups vegetable stock

Method:

1. Place a large skillet pan over medium-high heat, add 2 tablespoons butter and when melted, add steaks slices in a single layer.
2. Let cook for 4 to 5 minutes or until nicely browned on all sides.
3. Then transfer steak slices to a plate and cook remaining steak slices in the same manner.
4. Add remaining butter to the pan and when melted, add onion and garlic.

5. Let cook for 3 minutes or until fragrant.
6. Add mushrooms and continue cooking for 4 minutes.
7. Stir in paprika and mustard and then pour in broth.
8. Stir in lemon juice and bring the mixture to boil.
9. Let boil for 3 minutes and then stir in browned steak slices along with sour cream.
10. Remove pan from heat, garnish with parsley and ladle soup into bowls to serve.

Chicken Fajita Soup

Servings: 8 bowls.
Preparation time: 10 minutes
Cooking time: 6 hours and 30 minutes
Total time: 6 hours and 40 minutes

Nutrition Value:
Calories: 315 Cal, Carbs: 8.2 g, Net Carbs: 6.6 g, Fat: 17.6 g, Protein: 27.7 g.

Ingredients:

- 32-ounce chicken breasts
- 1 green pepper, chopped
- ½ cup chopped cilantro
- 20-ounce diced tomatoes with green chilies
- 1 medium-sized white onion, peeled and chopped
- 1 ½ teaspoon minced garlic
- 1 teaspoon salt
- ¾ teaspoon ground black pepper
- 2 ½ tablespoons taco seasoning
- 6-ounce cream cheese
- 1 tablespoon unsalted butter
- ½ cup heavy whipping cream
- 3 ½ cups chicken broth

Method:

1. Place chicken breast in a 6-quart slow cooker, season with salt and black pepper to taste and then cover with its lid.
2. Let cook for 3 hours on high heat setting or for 6 hours on low heat setting until cooked through.
3. When done, remove chicken from slow cooker and shred using forks.

4. Place a large saucepan over medium heat, add butter and when melted, add onion, garlic and green pepper.
5. Let cook for 3 to 4 minutes or until softened and then gradually stir in cream cheese until well combined.
6. Add tomatoes, taco seasoning, cream and chicken broth and stir until incorporated.
7. Reduce heat to low and simmer soup for 20 minutes, uncovering pot.
8. When done, taste soup to adjust seasoning and ladle soup into bowls.
9. Garnish with cilantro and serve.

Taco Soup

Servings: 8 bowls.
Preparation time: 10 minutes
Cooking time: 4 hours and 10 minutes
Total time: 4 hours and 20 minutes

Nutrition Value:
Calories: 73 Cal, Carbs: 11.3 g, Net Carbs: 9.2 g, Fat: 2.4 g, Protein: 2.1 g, Fiber: 2.1 g.

Ingredients:

- 32-ounces ground beef
- 20-ounce diced tomatoes with green chilies
- 1 teaspoon salt
- 1 teaspoon ground black pepper
- 1 tablespoons red chili powder
- ¼ teaspoon red pepper flakes
- 2 teaspoons cumin
- ¼ teaspoon dried oregano
- ½ teaspoon paprika
- ¼ cup heavy whipping cream
- 16-ounce cream cheese
- 3 cups beef broth

Method:

1. Place a large pan over medium heat, add beef and let cook for 7 to 10 minutes or until nicely brown.
2. When done, spoon beef into a 6-quart slow cooker.
3. Add remaining ingredients and stir until well combined.
4. Cover slow cooker with its lid and let cook for 4 hours on the low heat setting.
5. When done, ladle soup into serving bowl and serve.

CHAPTER 15: DESSERTS

Macadamia Nut Fat Bomb

Servings: 6 fat bombs.
Preparation time: 30 minutes
Cooking time: 0 minutes
Total time: 30 minutes

Nutrition Value:
Calories: 292 Cal, Carbs: 2 g, Net Carbs: 1 g, Fat: 40 g, Protein: 4 g, Fiber: 1 g.

Ingredients:

- 12 macadamia nuts
- 2 tablespoons cocoa powder, unsweetened
- 1/8 teaspoon salt
- 2 tablespoons Swerve sweetener
- 1 teaspoon vanilla extract, unsweetened
- 1/3 cup coconut oil, melted

Method:

1. Place cocoa, sweetener, vanilla, and oil in a bowl and whisk until smooth.
2. Take a small container, line with parchment sheet, then pour in prepared chocolate mixture, spread evenly and smooth the top using a spatula.
3. Scatter with macadamia nuts and sprinkle with salt.
4. Place this container for 20 minutes in the refrigerator until set.
5. Then remove the container from the refrigerator and cut into 6 squares.
6. Serve immediately or store in the refrigerator.

Chocolate Mousse

Servings: 4.
Preparation time: 40 minutes
Cooking time: 0 minutes
Total time: 40 minutes

Nutrition Value:
Calories: 137.5 Cal, Carbs: 4 g, Net Carbs: 4 g, Fat: 12 g, Protein: 1 g, Fiber: 0 g.

Ingredients:

- ¼ cup blueberries, frozen
- ½ cup cauliflower, frozen
- ½ medium-sized avocado
- 2/3 cup coconut milk unsweetened
- 2 scoops Exogenous Ketones, chocolate flavor
- 2 tablespoons swerve sweetener
- 2 tablespoons cocoa powder, unsweetened
- 1 teaspoon vanilla extract, unsweetened
- 1 teaspoon cinnamon
- 1/8 teaspoon salt

Method:

1. Place all the ingredients in a blender and pulse for 2 to 3 minutes or until smooth.
2. Tip the mousse in a bowl and let chill for 30 minutes in the refrigerator.
3. Serve chilled with sliced fruits.

Mug Cake

Servings: 1.
Preparation time: 5 minutes
Cooking time: 15 minutes
Total time: 20 minutes

Nutrition Value:
Calories: 296.6 Cal, Carbs: 5.6 g, Net Carbs: 2.3 g, Fat: 21.9 g, Protein: 9.6 g, Fiber: 3.3 g.

Ingredients:

- 2 tablespoons cocoa powder, unsweetened
- ½ teaspoon baking powder
- ¼ teaspoon salt
- 2 tablespoons swerve sweetener
- 1 scoop Keto Collagen
- 1 tablespoon sunflower butter
- 2 eggs
- 2 tablespoons coconut milk, unsweetened

Method:

1. Crack eggs in a large mug and whisk in butter and milk until smooth.
2. Stir in cocoa powder, baking powder and salt until combined and mix collagen using a fork.
3. Place mug into microwave and let microwave for 2 minutes at high heat setting.
4. When done, carefully remove mug from the oven and let cool for 15 minutes.
5. Serve immediately.

Avocado Vanilla Pudding

Servings: 4 chicken breasts.
Preparation time: 35 minutes
Cooking time: 0 minutes
Total time: 40 minutes

Nutrition Value:
Calories: 292 Cal, Carbs: 5.8 g, Net Carbs: 3.8 g, Fat: 28.8 g, Protein: 23.9 g, Fiber: 2 g, Salt: 17 mg, Cholesterol: 0 mg.

Ingredients:

- 14-ounces coconut milk, unsweetened
- 1 tablespoon lime juice
- 80 drops of liquid stevia
- 2 teaspoons vanilla extract, unsweetened
- 2 medium-sized avocados, peeled and cored

Method:

1. Cut avocado into bite-sized pieces and add to a blender.
2. Add remaining ingredients and pulse for 2 to 3 minutes or until smooth and creamy.
3. Tip pudding into a serving bowl, let chill for 30 minutes before serving.

Coconut Bars

Servings: 20 bars.
Preparation time: 55 minutes
Cooking time: 0 minutes
Total time: 55 minutes

Nutrition Value:
Calories: 108 Cal, Carbs: 2 g, Net Carbs: 0 g, Fat: 11 g, Protein: 3 g, Fiber: 2 g, Salt: 0 mg, Cholesterol: 7 mg.

Ingredients:

- 3 cups shredded coconut, unsweetened
- 1/4 cup liquid stevia
- 1 cup coconut oil, melted

Method:

1. Take a loaf pan or square baking pan, 8 by 8 inch, then line it with parchment sheet and set aside until required.
2. Place coconut in a large bowl and gradually mix in stevia and oil until well mixed.
3. Stir in water if the mixture is too crumbly and then spoon this mixture into prepared pan.
4. Press mixture into the pan using wet fingers and then place pan into the freezer.
5. Let chill for 45 minutes or until firm.
6. Then take out the mixture, cut into bars and serve.

No Bake Cookies

Servings: 18 cookies.
Preparation time: 20 minutes
Cooking time: 0 minutes
Total time: 20 minutes

Nutrition Value:
Calories: 174 Cal, Carbs: 6 g, Net Carbs: 3.2 g, Fat: 16.1 g, Protein: 5 g, Fiber: 2.8 g, Salt: 88.4 mg, Cholesterol: 6.7 mg.

Ingredients:

- 1 cup shredded coconut, unsweetened
- 1 tablespoon cocoa powder, unsweetened
- 4 drops stevia, vanilla flavored
- 2 tablespoons unsalted butter
- 2/3 cup peanut butter, organic

Method:

1. Place butter in a bowl and let melt in the microwave.
2. Then stir in peanut butter until well combined and then stir in cocoa powder until mixed.
3. Add shredded coconut and stevia until mixed well.
4. Take a medium-sized baking sheet, lined with parchment sheet and then place scoops in prepared cookies dough.
5. Place the baking sheet into the freezer for 10 minutes or until freeze and hard.
6. When done, serve cookies straight away or store in refrigerator in a sealed plastic bag.

Chocolate Bark with Bacon and Almonds

Servings: 8.
Preparation time: 30 minutes
Cooking time: 2 minutes
Total time: 32 minutes

Nutrition Value:
Calories: 157 Cal, Carbs: 2 g, Net Carbs: 5.2 g, Fat: 12.8 g, Protein: 4 g, Fiber: 7.5 g, Salt: 21 mg, Cholesterol: 16 mg.

Ingredients:

- 2 slices of bacon, cooked and crumbled
- ½ cup chopped almonds
- 9-ounce baking chips, dark chocolate flavored

Method:

1. Place baking chips in a microwave ovenproof bowl and let heat for 30 seconds at high heat settings.
2. Then stir and continue microwave for 30 seconds.
3. Stir again and microwave for 15 seconds or until chocolate chips are completely melted.
4. Fold in almonds into melted chocolate mixture.
5. Take a baking sheet, line with parchment sheet and spoon in prepared chocolate mixture.
6. Spread mixture as thinly as possible, about ½-inch thick, and then scatter crumbled bacon on top.
7. Press bacon pieces into chocolate using a spatula and then place baking sheet into the refrigerator.
8. Let chill for 20 minutes or until hard.
9. Then break chocolate into 8 pieces.
10. Serve straight away or store in the refrigerator.

Lemon Bars

Servings: 8 bars.
Preparation time: 15 minutes
Cooking time: 45 minutes
Total time: 1 hour

Nutrition Value:
Calories: 272 Cal, Carbs: 4.7 g, Net Carbs: 4 g, Fat: 263 g, Protein: 8 g, Fiber: 0.7 g, Salt: 34 mg, Cholesterol: 8 mg.

Ingredients:

- 1 ¾ cups almond flour
- ¼ teaspoon salt
- 1 cup erythritol, powdered
- ½ cup unsalted butter, melted
- 3 lemons, zested and juiced
- 3 eggs

Method:

1. Set oven to 350 degrees F and let preheat.
2. In the meantime, place 1 cup flour in a large bowl and stir in 1/8 teaspoon salt and ¼ cup erythritol until combined.
3. Take a loaf pan or a square baking pan, about 8 by 8 inch, and spoon in the prepared dough.
4. Press dough into pan using wet finger and then place pan into the oven.
5. Let bake for 20 minutes, then remove the pan from oven and let cool for 10 minutes on wire rack.
6. Meanwhile, place lemon juice and lemon zest in a bowl and crack eggs along with remaining flour, erythritol and salt.
7. Stir until well combined and then pour this mixture evenly over baked almond flour crust.

8. Return pan to oven and continue baking for 25 minutes or until top is nicely brown and set.
9. When done, take out crust, then let cool for 15 minutes and sprinkle with erythritol.
10. Slice to serve.

Conclusion

This book aimed to educate the readers about how to successfully implement this diet and bring about a positive change in one's lifestyle. All beginners have fears that are understandable and their questions are respected. The FAQs 'Chapter 8' is sure to help anyone who is finding it hard to muster up the courage to start.

The low carb, high-fat philosophy is new to people, but it is getting recognition very quickly as it is reaping commendable results. The usual problem with diets is that people find it hard to resists cravings and do not feel full, but this diet gives a lot of liberty to its follower to consume the fat they need and there is no need to constantly watch calories either.

Hope that this keto journey brings a nice and refreshing change in your life!

Made in the USA
San Bernardino, CA
22 January 2019